35,00

THE

SERIES

Vol. 1	CHEVROLET: The Coming of Age	1911-1942
Vol. 2	CHEVROLET: USA # 1	1946-1959
Vol. 3	The Real CORVETTE	Chevy's Sports Car

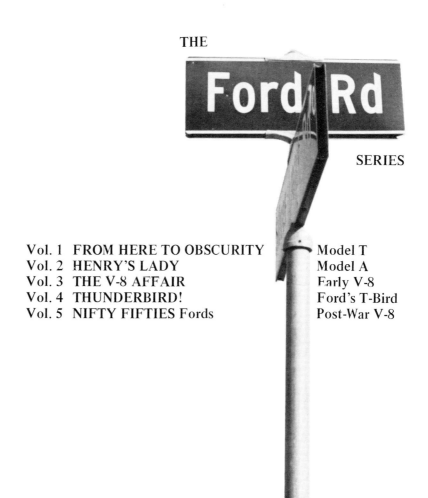

THE

SERIES

Vol. 1	FROM HERE TO OBSCURITY	Model T
Vol. 2	HENRY'S LADY	Model A
Vol. 3	THE V-8 AFFAIR	Early V-8
Vol. 4	THUNDERBIRD!	Ford's T-Bird
Vol. 5	NIFTY FIFTIES Fords	Post-War V-8

CHEVROLET: U·S·A·1

An Illustrated History of Chevrolet's Passenger Cars

1946-1959

By RAY MILLER

THE EVERGREEN PRESS
Oceanside, California

CHEVROLET: USA #1
an illustrated history of Chevrolet's Passenger Cars

First Printing: May 1977
Third Printing: Feb. 1980

Library of Congress Catalog Card #76-12000

ISBNO-913056-07-3

Copyright Ray Miller 1977

Printed by:
    Sierra Printers, Inc.
    Bakersfield, California

Printed in U.S.A.

The Evergreen Press
Box 1711
Oceanside, California 92054

RAY MILLER, along with Bruce McCalley, another Founding Member of the Model T Ford Club of America, produced FROM HERE TO OBSCURITY, a book that has become the Standard Reference for those interested in the Model T Ford. From there, it was a relatively modest effort for him to turn his talents to coverage of the Model A, and with Glenn Embree, he produced HENRY'S LADY and THE V-8 AFFAIR, a similar work covering the pre-war Ford V-8. Following this came THUNDERBIRD! and the NIFTY FIFTIES. The work has been assembled as THE FORD ROAD SERIES, the five volumes of which have been described as "the greatest collection of detailed information" on the Ford Automobile.

A subsequent book, the Real CORVETTE, joined CHEVROLET: The Coming of Age, published earlier, and this latest effort, CHEVROLET: USA #1, and are assembled as THE CHEVY CHASE SERIES, the three volumes of which detail the annual model changes in the products of the Chevrolet Motor Division from its inception through the 1959 model year.

Ray has been interested in cars for many years. In the past he has owned many Chevrolets as well as Fords, but of them all, he remembers best "tooling around all of one summer in a battered '56 'Vette". In contemporary times, he also has owned a 1958 Chevrolet Impala Sport Coupe and a 1959 Parkwood Station Wagon. At present his collection, limited only by available storage space, includes a 1910 Model T Ford, a 1936 Phaeton, '57 Thunderbird, a 1941 Lincoln Continental Coupe, and his "modern" car, a 1954 Skyliner in which he pursues his daily efforts.

In addition to having had the responsibility for the text and the production of this book, including the photographs, it was Ray who located the fine cars used to illustrate his work. His ability to find exactly the right cars, clearly demonstrated in the past, is enhanced by the fact that in Southern California there are still so very many original, unrestored, and un-modified cars being driven daily on the freeways.

The Author wishes to thank those who contributed their time and enthusiasm to make this book possible.

The Owners, generally mentioned by name within the text of this book are again thanked for their patient understanding of the needs of this photographer. It was so often necessary that the cars be moved, relocated for better effect, yet during all of the production of this book, never did we hear a complaint. Owners allowed us access to the interiors of their cars and welcomed our detailed photographic inspections. For this attitude, and for the many considerations that they gave us, we wish again to express our appreciation.

RJM

In preparing this materials, the author has attempted to locate unrestored, low mileage, original cars wherever possible. When failing in this he has employed as models restorations which are believed to be of the highest quality.

As is to be expected, there may well be items of incorrect date or style on a given automobile. Original cars may well have been modified to suit the convenience of an earlier owner; restorations are generally done to the best level of information available to the restorer, but occasionally a slip-up, sometimes of frightening proportions will occur.

We have *attempted* to screen the inaccuracies; we trust that we have succeeded in the effort. This book was intended to be what it is, a compendium of information which will enable an observer to identify, and to classify, both cars and parts. If there are errors, they are not to our knowledge.

1958 Brookwood Station Wagon

Glenn Embree, well-known Photographer, had been engaged by Chevrolet to obtain many of the excellent photographs employed in their advertising and promotional efforts. His work completed, Glenn had retained some of the unused transparencies in his files, and almost twenty years later was able, with characteristic generosity, to provide the author with these representative samples.

These photographs were taken in 1957 and 1958, and are prime examples of the skills of a foremost Photographic Illustrator. Although each incorporates a familiar scenario, the people involved are subdued and there can be no question of the intent of the photograph. Each emphatically illustrates the undeniable excitement that these Chevrolets provide.

1957 Bel Air Convertible

1957 Bel Air Sport Sedan

On a sunny day in San Diego, California, Chevrolets representing the years of 1955, 1956, and 1957 assemble to be photographed.

Alfred P. Sloan, Jr. President of General Motors from May 10, 1923 until his retirement at the age of 71 in 1946.

When he assumed the Presidency of General Motors in May of 1923, he was presented with an amalgamation of independently-acting automotive vehicle and parts manufacturing enterprises of which none was currently directed towards challenging Ford, by far the leading manufacturer of low-priced automobiles.

Convinced that his Company's future required the manufacture of "a car for every purse and purpose", he rejected the recommendation of experts that he dismantle his unprofitable Chevrolet division, and caused it to direct its entire energies towards production of a car specifically intended to supplant the ubiquitous Model T Ford.

Important as they were, his greatest contribution to General Motors may not have been establishing the permanent Corporate Structure, or his brilliant concept of an Annual Model Change, but it may well be his determination to topple the Leader and establish Chevrolet as USA #1.

To Alfred P. Sloan, Jr., is this book respectfully dedicated.

The '56 Chevrolet

It looks high priced—but it's the new Chevrolet "Two-Ten" 4-Door Sedan.

For sooner and safer arrivals!

It's so nimble and quick on the road . . .

Of course, you don't have to have an urgent errand and a motorcycle escort to make use of Chevrolet's quick and nimble ways. Wherever you go, the going's sweeter and safer in a Chevy.

Power's part of the reason. Chevrolet's horse-power ranges up to 205. And these numbers add up to *action*—second-saving acceleration for safer passing . . . rapid-fire reflexes that help you avoid trouble before it happens!

True, lots of cars are high powered today, but the difference is in the way Chevrolet *handles* its power. It's rock-steady on the road . . . clings to curves like part of the pavement. That's *stability*—and it helps make Chevrolet one of the few great road cars!

Highway-test one, soon. Your Chevrolet dealer will be happy to arrange it. . . . Chevrolet Division of General Motors, Detroit 2, Mich.

THE HOT ONE'S EVEN HOTTER

Traffic-test it—it's a beautiful thing to handle!

In presenting his material, the Author has made no attempt to isolate the cars except by model year. Since we have been attempting to describe the *characteristics* of a given year, we have deliberately employed those pictures which best served the immediate purpose. *For this reason, adjacent photos may not necessarily show views of the same car.*

CONTENTS

*A*lthough its antecedents now seem frequently to be confused, the present Chevrolet Division of the General Motors Corporation was started, (perhaps vindictively), by William C. Durant in 1910 following his ouster from an earlier organization which he had also founded, the General Motors Corporation. Durant had been a high flyer, a man of great, boundless, enthusiasm, who had over-extended both himself and his company.

On his ouster he engaged the services of race driver Louis Chevrolet, formerly an employee of his at GM, to design and build a car to be manufactured and built by a new company. Liking the melodious sound of the name, Durant decided to name his new effort the Chevrolet Motor Company and, although Louis Chevrolet was a participant in the ownership, it was only of relatively few shares.

A subsequent disagreement between the two men regarding the type of automobile that would have to be built by Chevrolet Motor Company resulted in the departure from the company of Louis Chevrolet, but his name remained, and the Company prospered under Durant's able guidance. Building a small, four-cylinder light car that was successful in the market,

Durant was able to acquire with his earnings and via stock trade, a controlling interest in General Motors in only six years. Chevrolet Motor Company did, in truth, control GM, and Durant controlled Chevrolet.

Later, in a logical move that seems to be a reverse action, the shares of Chevrolet were sold to General Motors and the assets of the former folded into the GM activity. Obviously a means by which his stock ownership of Chevrolet could be "cashed out", it has nevertheless led to the incorrect assumption that GM "bought" Chevrolet; actually, at the time of acquisition, Chevrolet was clearly in control of the larger Company.

In any event, Chevrolet Motor Company thus became the Chevrolet Motor Division of GM and has so remained since 1918. It has supplanted Buick and Cadillac as the major activity of the Corporation, and continues to be the bellwether of that organization. Chevrolet was assigned by later Corporate Management to attract and hold a major share of the automobile market and to an unquestioned extent has succeeded in its assignment.

The 1942 Special De Luxe 5-passenger Coupe, produced in limited numbers before the war interrupted production, was of the first model year to introduce the new longer fenders extending onto the doors.

Under Government edict certain metals had been declared essential and unavailable for civilian use, and by January of 1942, all remaining civilian passenger car production was halted, with the last Chevrolet passenger car assembled on January 30th at Flint.

The following three and a half years were active years at GM. With most of the able-bodied young men in the army, women were moved into the plants to work on the production lines and it is to the credit of the Company that thousands of critical weapons and supplies were produced under trying conditions. The Chevrolet Division is noted for its production of military trucks, ammunition, the Pratt & Whitney aircraft engine, and other items, but the end of hostilities arrived and, on October 3, 1945, the *first* post-war Chevrolet passenger car was assembled.

The 1942 Chevrolet was principally innovative for its use of "caps" on the doors to extend the apparent length of the front fenders, and the design was carried forward on the 1946 model. With the end of the war came a huge, and predictable, demand for civilian automobiles and the 1942 tooling was dusted off and returned to production. Only relatively minor cosmetic changes were made in the haste to get production rolling again, yet sadly, a bitter labor strike limited production of the 1946 models produced in 1945 to just over 12,000 units, (the model year closed at well over 400,000 though with most activity in calendar 1946.)

The 1946 models greatly resembled the earlier 1942 versions. Front end treatment differed however, and the radiator grill was redesigned and parking lamps relocated.

1946 Stylemaster Sport Sedan

During the early post-war period, Chevrolet, like Ford, continued to produce a modified version of its immediate pre-war 1942 model. The market was demanding transportation, not improved style and other evolutionary features, and backlogs were going up, not down, despite the production of hundreds of thousands of "obsolescent" cars. Despite their sale of over 400,000 1946 models, Chevrolet announced in February of 1947 that its backlog was "25% *higher* than a year ago", and that new orders were being accepted "on a long range basis only".

The very active black market in automobiles operated almost openly and it was no secret to anyone that a cash payment "under the table" in addition to the stated contract price could assure the delivery of a car. Strangely, the mood and the morals of the Country were such that there seemed to be no quarrel with this operation, only with the size of the cash payment!

By 1948, despite the fact that the model was again substantially identical to the 1946, having had only cosmetic changes, Chevrolet found itself still selling every car that it could produce. In February, an article in The *New York Times* reported that "Buyers *not* wanting "extras" reported to be waiting 15 months for a car", and the manufacturers and dealers continued to add unwanted "extras" like hill-holders, special polishes, cleaners, and grill guards . . thus inflating the selling prices.

Resuming car production in October of 1945, Chevrolet was quick to place advertisements extolling their claim to First Place in production for ten of the preceeding eleven years of production.

In 1948, the automotive market was shaken with the introduction of a totally new model by Studebaker, the first true post-war design. The "Big Three", General Motors, Ford, and Chrysler had to respond in kind. This was to be the last year in which their pre-war style would be produced. Starting in 1949, the distinctive ideas of their excellent Styling, Design, and Engineering staffs would enter the production lines and their first post-war cars would emerge.

The new models scored, along with the new assembly plants that had been opened in Flint and Los Angeles in 1947, and for 1949, Chevrolet's sales leaped to over one million units, a jump of one third over 1948, reaching a level of 21.6% of the total market.

"Chevrolet Is First", again announced in their advertisement in the Ladies Home Journal in May of 1948, repeats the familiar theme.

The Pace Car for the annual 500 mile race at Indianapolis in May was this sporty 1948 Chevrolet Fleetmaster Convertible.

By the summer of 1951, Chevrolet subtlely entered into their advertising the clarion call to the Road: "See the U.S.A. In your Chevrolet". This excellent promotional slogan was to become the sign-off exhortation of Dinah Shore on her popular Sunday evening TV variety show which was sponsored by Chevrolet.

Although the conventional car advertisements for Chevrolets during 1953 were comparatively bland (right), something new was brewing at Chevrolet in the form of a unique new American Sports Car. The prototype Corvette conceived as a "dream car" was first displayed in January of 1953. By 1954 the car had been placed in production and has remained there to the present. Readers are invited to review "The Real CORVETTE", also by the author, for the full story of the marque.

Through 1952, Chevrolet's car continued to be offered in only two lines, first available in 1949, the Special and the De Luxe. Powerglide, an automatic transmission, was introduced in 1950 along with an up-rated six-cylinder "Blue Flame" engine. Also introduced in 1950 was the Bel Air, a two-door "hardtop convertible", a style-setter for virtually every other manufacturer for years to come.

1953 models introduced the one-piece curved windshield, and a return to the three-series concept including the 150, the 210, and the top of the line Bel Air series. Aluminum pistons were introduced in some 1953 engines and became standard in all in 1954.

Despite the continued up-grading, and their substantial marketing success, Chevrolet sought to associate with itself an aura of youthful and sporting appearance. Since the success of Chevrolet, to begin with, seems to lie with their highly successful effort to define the *average* buyer and produce to suit his desires, this was a curous pursuit. However, during 1953, Chevrolet placed into limited production their exciting new American Sports Car, the Corvette. Utilizing off-the-shelf components to a large extent, including the sturdy Blue Flame six-cylinder engine and Powerglide, only 300 were produced, most in the last quarter of the year, all virtually hand-fabricated at Flint. By January 1st, production was moved to St. Louis where it has remained until the present.

1955 was the bell-ringer! For the first time in 34 years, Chevrolet had a V-8 engine, together with restyled bodies that were true style-setters. Chevrolet soared, rising by almost 500,000 units over 1954.

Photo courtesy of The Flint Journal

On November 22, 1954, GM and the city of Flint staged a parade to commemorate manufacture of the 50,000,000th General Motors car. Designated for the honor was this gold colored 1955 Bel Air Sport Coupe which was specially outfitted with many gold-plated parts. Thousands of people lined the streets to watch the milestone car pass by.

Again in 1955, Chevrolet was selected to provide the Pace Car at the annual 500 mile race at the Indianapolis Speedway.

A then-obscure race driver, Zora Arkus-Duntov, later to become a dominant force behind the success of the Chevrolet Corvette, set a stock car record on Pikes Peak in this pre-production 1956 Chevrolet. His record of just over 17 minutes stood for 13 years before Bobby Unser, using another Chevrolet, lowered it by 30%.

SHOW STOPPER

SINCE WAY BACK WHEN !

Chevrolet has been "stopping the show" ever since the 1927 model pictured above came on the scene. That year, incidentally, marked the beginning of Chevrolet's popularity leadership, and over the entire period since then, Chevrolet has been America's first choice car.

You'll see why Chevrolet is stopping the show again this year when you visit the General Motors Motorama. You'll see the beautiful new Chevrolet for 1954—the car that's Powered for *Performance!* . . . Engineered for *Economy!* You'll learn firsthand about all the wonderful new features offered by America's favorite car. And you'll see sensational "Cars of the future"— Chevrolet experimental models—the Corvair, the Nomad and the Chevrolet Corvette Convertible Coupe.

Be sure to come in and see these and other exciting attractions at the General Motors Motorama—the most talked about show of them all!

THE CHEVROLET NOMAD
Here for the first time is an experimental model combining the sleek styling of a sports car with the versatility and utility of a six-passenger Station Wagon. The body is of glass fiber reinforced plastic construction

THE CHEVROLET CORVAIR
Here in this experimental two-passenger model with its glass fiber reinforced plastic body, Chevrolet brings new aerodynamic design to the closed sports car. The ultra-streamlined top sweeps back to a jet exhaust-type rear opening.

THE CHEVROLET CORVETTE CONVERTIBLE COUPE
The sports car gains new all-weather utility in this new experimental model. The *removable top*—of the same glass fiber plastic construction as the body itself—may be left behind in the garage on warm days.

CHEVROLET
on display at the General Motors
MOTORAMA

CIVIC AUDITORIUM • MARCH 27 through APRIL 4 ADMISSION FREE
ADMISSION FREE
OPEN UNTIL 11:00 P.M. EVERY DAY • SUNDAY from NOON • ALL OTHER DAYS from 10 A.M.

The Motorama was an all-GM show intended to stimulate interest in the products of all of the divisions. It was held in the Spring of each year starting in New York City in January and visiting other major cities including Miami, Los Angeles, San Francisco, Dallas, etc. In a special 12 page supplement to the San Francisco Chronicle on May 28, 1954, Chevrolet's ad featured a celebrated name (Corvair) yet to be employed on the later rear-engined car, an experimental hard top (which never entered production) for their early Corvette, and the new Nomad built to resemble the lines of the 1954 Corvette.

Chevrolet had an interestisng idea. A two-door station wagon with a fold-down rear seat and a touch of elegance. Perceived as the answer for what they saw as a market for this hybrid, Chevrolet confused the competition by building their prototype sports car/wagon to resemble their Corvette (right). Built however on a station wagon chassis (not the Corvette chassis), it was first shown in the 1953 Motorama (opposite page), but actually entered production in the revised now-familiar sheet metal seen below.

The Nomad shown in the 1955 Motorama display (below) had design refinements which included a sharper and crisper fender and rear styling, and entered production early in 1955.

Although the Nomads of 1955-57 have become strong collectors' items, they were actually not well received, Chevrolet having over-estimated the demand for such vehicles. The name was continued on a dress-up four-door wagon, but after 1957, the interesting two-door model was discontinued with a total of only about 23,000 having been built for the entire three year run.

for Economical Transportation
CHEVROLET

1914 Baby Grand Touring

Early Baby Grand Touring car was 4-cylinder engine version of still earlier Classic Six, a heavy, larger car designed by Louis Chevrolet.

1919 490 Touring

New low-priced 490, introduced in 1916 at $490, was aimed at low-price car market.

1927 Capitol Coach

1927 Coach was extremely popular version of the early Chevrolet and featured a steering column lock.

1929 International Sport Cabriolet

1929 model introduced an advanced new six-cylinder engine which was promoted as a "six for the price of four".

1932 DeLuxe Sport Roadster

1932 De Luxe Sport Roadster featured six wire wheels and the unforgetable "doors" in the hood sides.

By 1938, Chevrolet had a curiously modern appearance which was to remain popular for several years.

1938 Master Town Sedan

1941 Special De Luxe Five Passenger Coupe

The 1941 model was first to eliminate the outside running boards, and used a new wider body shell which offered more inside room.

By early 1942, when production was interrupted by the War, critical metal shortages and Government regulations had eliminated almost all chromed trim.

1942 Master De Luxe Business Coupe (Black-out version)

1946

1947

1948

1949

1950

1951

1952

1953

1954

1955

1956

1957

1958

1959

1946

Based almost entirely on the 1942 model, the immediate post-war Chevrolet displayed very little that was "new". The grill was re-styled slightly, the parking lamps were relocated, and chrome-plated trim items returned to replace much of the prewar plastic, but Chevrolet's main claims for 1946 were the fact that their "Knee-Action, valve-in-head engine, Synchro-Mesh transmission and all other mechanical units are identical in design and construction with those used in the Chevrolet chassis before the war".

What was _new_ however, were the names. The 1942 Master De Luxe series became the new Stylemaster (DJ) Series, and the old Special De Luxe was now the Fleetmaster (DK) Series. Still considered a sub-series in the Fleetmaster line was the fancy Fleetline group which featured both a four-door Sportsmaster sedan and the popular two-door Aerosedan.

All cars were built on a 116" wheel base, introduced in 1941, and used the familiar 216 cubic inch six cylinder engine.

PROVED VALVE-IN-HEAD THRIFT-MASTER ENGINE

No other car in the lowest-priced group has a valve-in-head engine—the type used in Chevrolet. It's the valve-in-head principle that has made Chevrolet's 90-horsepower six-cylinder engine famous for its rare combination of economy and performance—because the valve-in-head engine is the most efficient type known to engineering. Here, truly, is the Thrift-Master, because it does more work per unit of fuel consumed, and therefore requires less fuel to equal the performance of a conventional engine of the same displacement.

1946 Stylemaster Sport Coupe

1946 Fleetline Aerosedan

Bob Matheson, Renton, Washington

Below the distinctive winged insignia, the effect of wide horizontal grill bars is diminished by a downward-turned frame which gives the car a somewhat narrow appearance.

The Chevrolet name is placed on the bottom grill bar.

The parking lights have been relocated to a new protected position at the bottom of the grill. Accessory bumper ends, as seen on this car, give added protection but conceal the lights somewhat.

Fog lamps are an accessory which mounts to the bumper brackets through the front splash apron.

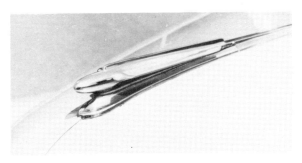

The hood ornament is slim and modern.

The headlamps are faired nicely into the fenders.

Headlight doors are painted, not chromed. Lamps are sealed beams, six volt.

First introduced on the 1942 models, fender "caps" are placed on the front doors giving the fenders a longer and more graceful appearance.

Wheels are 16 inch diameter, and tires are 600:16. One stripe appears on the wheel. Whitewall tires were not available in 1946, but wide white plastic beauty rings (not shown) were offered as accessories.

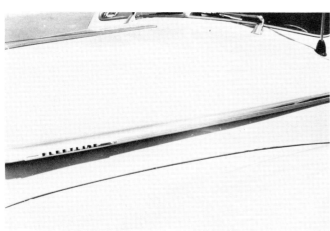

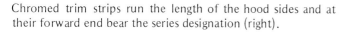

Chromed trim strips run the length of the hood sides and at their forward end bear the series designation (right).

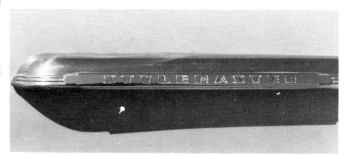

The set of three graceful trim stripes at the bottom of the front (left) and rear fenders appear only on the Fleetline models. Fleetmaster and Stylemaster cars do not have them (below).

The bright metal trim around the windshield is omitted on the lower-priced Stylemaster line.

When the accessory radio is installed, its antenna is located on the left side of the cowl.

A cowl vent is supplied as an aid to cooling the interior.

Dual windshield wipers are furnished on all models.

A rare accessory is this windshield washer located on the cowl.

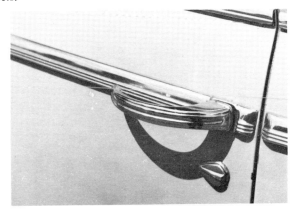

The appearance of the curved door handles is minimized by their location in the side trim stripe. Beneath them on each front door is an external lock.

The somewhat triangular rear quarter window of the Fleetline Aerosedan emphasizes the sloping roof lines of this model. These windows can be lowered about half way.

Vent windows are provided in the front doors of all models.

Rear fender stone guards are placed on all models.

The three bright metal trim strips on the fenders are unique to the Fleetline Areosedan and its companion, the four-door Fleetline Sportsmaster Sedan.

The sharply slanted rear window of the Aerosedan was considered by some drivers to limit their vision, but the style was extremely popular.

The spacious integral luggage compartment at the rear of the Aerosedan is reached by raising the lid which is internally hinged at its top. The back up lamp below the left tail light is an after-market accessory.

An attractive new combination trunk handle and license plate holder makes its appearance in 1946.

The tail lamps continue in the style first introduced in 1941.

The two outer bumper guards are standard, but the center one is an optional accessory. Note the embossed splash apron between the body and the bumper.

The dashboard of the 1946 is almost identical with that found in the 1942 models. This is a Fleetmaster series car; the Stylemaster cars had a somewhat more plain instrument panel and were furnished with a three-spoke steering wheel.

The Fleetmaster two-spoked steering wheel is fitted with this fancy horn button. Stylemaster series cars had a plainer button on their three-spoke wheel.

The original upholstery in the 1946 Aerosedan is pin-striped mohair.

The vent windows are locked with a sliding pin.

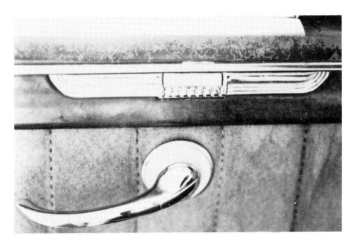

Window sills and the instrument panel, in Fleetmaster Series cars are wood-grained. Those in the Stylemaster series are painted.

Returning promptly are chromed metal window riser cranks and door handles replacing the brittle plastic type used in the 1942 cars.

Instrument panel layout of the 1946 models is unchanged from 1942. Fleetmaster series has bright-metal trim (which is omitted from the Stylemaster series) on the glove box door and surrounding the instruments at the left (see below). Heater is the economy model, a more elaborate Super De Luxe heater/defroster having been introduced in 1942.

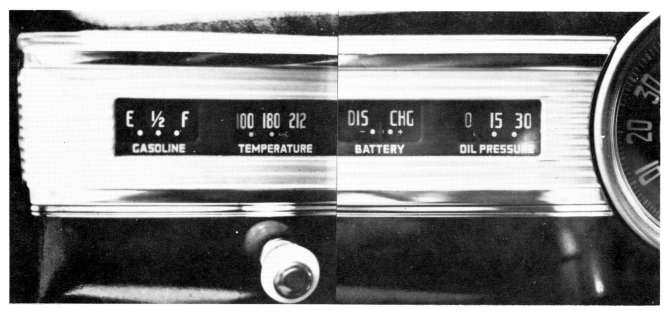

Instruments are unchanged from 1946. The bright bezel trim over these instruments is omitted on the Stylemaster series.

Dark face/light lettering instruments continue to be used. The "100 mph" speedometer rating was first used in 1934, and the resettable trip indicator found in early days was eliminated from the Chevrolet speedometers in 1933.

An ash tray is provided at the top center of the instrument panel. Below it, and under the lettered trim plate is the radio speaker grill on which is placed a decorative emblem.

At the bottom center of the instrument panel is the radio which is an optional accessory. This is a deluxe five push-button model. The large horizontal knob above the center push-button is employed to control the brightness of the radio dial light.

At the far left is the Throttle knob, and the radio volume control knob is to its right. Barely visible on the escutcheon plate of the radio knob are the letters V M B which relate to *V*oice, *M*usic, and *B*ass, since this is a tone control adjustment.

The clock face matches that of the speedometer. At its bottom, near the figure 6 is a reset knob.

Series EK   Fleetmaster Series
                   Sport Sedan (4-door)
                   Town Sedan (2-door)
                   Station Wagon
                   5-passenger Coupe
                   Cabriolet

                 Fleetline Series
                   Aerosedan (2-door)
                   Sportmaster (4-door)

Series EJ   Stylemaster Series
                   Sport Sedan (4-door)
                   3-passenger Business Coupe
                   5-passenger Sport Coupe
                   Town Sedan (2-door)

ENGINE
Chevrolet is the lowest-priced car offering the many advantages of valve-in-head engine design. The outstanding superiority of this type of engine is its higher efficiency, that is, its ability to accomplish more on a given quantity of fuel—or to perform any given task with less fuel—as compared with any other type of engine now in general use in motor vehicles.

UNITIZED KNEE-ACTION
The Chevrolet Big-Car ride is due to its highly developed front-end suspension. Each wheel is mounted, independent of the other, on an easy-action coil spring, and controlled by a built-in double-acting shock absorber. Both Knee-Action units, together with the front wheel mountings, brakes and steering connections, are carried on a massive cross-member. The whole front end is assembled, then adjusted and aligned, before being attached to the chassis as a unit.

Little change was made in the 1947 models. Foremost was a revision of the grill with the new horizontal bars softening the appearance of the front end. The horizontal trim stripe which ran from the hood to the rear on the 1946 models (page 31) was omitted on all models in 1947.

Specifications

ENGINE: Six cylinders, valve-in-head. Specialized 4-way oiling system. Single-adjustment downdraft carburetor, with air cleaner, silencer and flame arrester; 16-gallon fuel tank. Permanently lubricated water pump; full-length cylinder water jackets; coolant capacity, 15 quarts. Delco-Remy ignition, with automatic spark advance and octane selector; mechanical-shift starter. Diaphragm-spring clutch. Syncro-Mesh transmission, vacuum-power gearshift.

CHASSIS: Box-girder frame. Unitized Knee-Action, with ride stabilizer. Double-acting shock absorbers, front and rear. Hypoid-drive rear axle, ratio 4.11:1. Shockproof steering. Hydraulic brakes; self-aligning, full-contact brake shoes. Five steel disc wheels, 6.00-16 tires. Wheelbase, 116 inches. Bumper, two guards, front and rear.

ELECTRICAL: Sealed Beam headlamps, foot-controlled; two tail and stop lights (one on Station Wagon). Dual matched horns. 15-plate, 100-ampere-hour battery. Illuminated ignition lock.

ALL BODIES: No Draft ventilation. Concealed entrance steps. Foot scraper at each front door. Concealed door-hinges.

SEDANS AND COUPES: Fisher Unisteel construction; Turret Top and solid steel underbody. Safety plate glass throughout. Three-passenger adjustable front seat, full-width cushion (divided back in two-door sedans and coupes). Provision for heater installation under front seat. Pile fabric upholstery in *Stylemaster* and *Fleetmaster*; two-tone Bedford cord optional in *Fleetmaster*; non-pile "Fleetweave" fabric in *Fleetline*. Leatherette scuff covering on doors and front seats (also on rear seats of *Fleetmaster* and *Fleetline*.) Carpet inserts in front floor rubber mat (except *Stylemaster*). Two leather-topped front seat arm rests in *Fleetmaster* and *Fleetline*. Two adjustable sliding sun shades (one in *Stylemaster*). Radio grille. Package compartment with lock (illuminated in *Fleetmaster* and *Fleetline*).

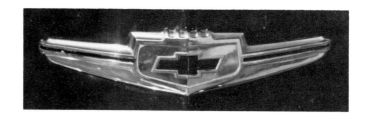

1947 Fleetmaster Station Wagon

Chevrolet introduced its wooden-bodied Station Wagon in 1939, a relatively late entry into the field (Ford had been building them since 1929). Chevrolet's pre-war wooden bodies were the products of sub-contractors, but commencing with the 1946 model, these bodies were built by General Motors itself.

Mr. Bill Halliday, Newport Beach, California

1947

A reconfigured front grill treatment provides a cleaner, and wider appearance.

Headlights remain unchanged, and are set into the front fenders as previously.

Parking lights are placed between the bottom two grill bars and are unchanged from the 1946 model.

A redesigned hood ornament appears for 1947.

Apparent width is added to the car by cleverly emphasizing with the grill bars the parting line of the hood.

Headlamp doors are unchanged and still bear the familiar five-stripe painted trim.

The horizontal grill bars extend over the front fenders, below the headlights, for greater effect.

Wheels remain at 16 inch diameter. Black-wall 600 x 16 tires were standard, and despite their good looks, whitewall tires were not yet available as options.

The soft top covering of the Station Wagon rolls over the steel sill above the windshield.

As on the other models, the Station Wagon's front fenders are given length by the use of a "cap" on the front doors.

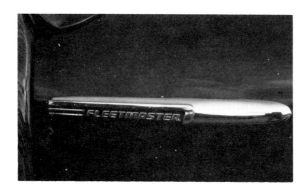

For 1947, the long horizontal body trim strip of 1946 has been eliminated and replaced with short longitudinal nameplates as seen here.

Windshield wipers are unchanged.

All models including the Station Wagon, have these rear fender gravel guards.

A lower body trim strip runs from the front fender to the front of the rear fender.

Chevrolet's wooden Station Wagon bodies are constructed of ash with mahogany panels. The top is of weatherproof grained leatherette stretched over wooden slats.

An inside door lock knob protrudes through the window sill.

The front doors are provided with keylocks located beneath the door handles.

The rear windows of the Station Wagon are sliding type and are locked with pins located at the posts. The gas tank filler tube is located on the right rear fender on all models except the Business Coupe.

Both front and rear doors are hinged at their forward edge (although front hinges are concealed), and open from the rear.

A two piece rear bumper is used to protect the rear-mounted spare wheel and a metal tire cover is supplied to dress up the appearance of the spare tire. The hub cap matches those on the other wheels.

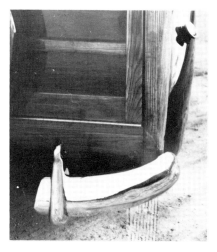

The single tail light/license plate holder is secured to the body on the rear left. The lamp assembly is hinged so that when the tail gate is lowered (opposite page), the lamp will shine to the rear.

The top is constructed with wooden slats screwed into the forward and rear bows and five cross-stringers. Over this is laid a muslin-like lining, a padding, and finally a long/short grain waterproof leatherette.

In addition to the expected dome light, the station wagon, like other models in the Fleetmaster line, has two sun visors. Stylemaster series cars have only one.

A T-handle locking knob secures the lift-gate which must be opened before the tailgate is dropped.

The liftgate is secured in the illustrated position by locking the guides at each end. The tail gate is dropped for access to the large storage area behind the passenger seat.

Two sheathed chains support the ends of the tail gate in the lowered position.

Chevrolet's vacuum-assist transmission gear shift permits shorter, easier, throw of the lever and is standard on all models.

The Fleetmaster steering wheel continues as a two-spoke wheel with full-circle horn blowing ring. Stylemaster cars have a three-spoke wheel and no horn ring.

The hub of the Fleetmaster cars is decorated with this insignia. Stylemaster horn buttons are somewhat plainer.

1947 Fleetmaster instrument panel

The two windshield wipers are operated by a single vacuum motor beneath the cowl controlled by this knob on the instrument panel.

A built-in ash receptacle is placed at the top center of the instrument panel in all models.

The radio speaker grill is standard in all models although the radio itself is an accessory. Above grill, the familiar Chevrolet "bow tie" insignia continues to appear.

Instruments displaying conditions of fuel level, temperature, battery charge, and oil pressure, are located to the left of the speedometer.

The radio is an accessory, and when not ordered, a cut-out portion of the instrument panel is sealed with an appropriate blanking panel.

To the left of the radio volume control (note the V M B positions of its concentric tone control) is the manual Throttle, and beyond that the ignition lock.

To the right of the radio tuning knob is the Choke control knob, and beyond it is a cigarette lighter, standard in Fleetline and Fleetmaster models.

An electric clock, optional in the Stylemaster Series, its face matching that of the speedometer, is located at the right side of the instrument panel. The package compartment located to its right is lighted on the Fleetmaster and Fleetline cars only.

Chromed handles with two-tone knobs on the window cranks, are featured.

All models have vent windows in the front doors which are operated by handcranks (below). The vents on the Station Wagon and Convertible are shaped differently than those on other models.

1948

Series F K   Fleetmaster
Sport Sedan (4-door)
Town Sedan (2-door)
Club Coupe
Cabriolet
Station Wagon
Fleetline Aerosedan (2-door)
Fleetline Sportmaster (4-door)

Series F J   Stylemaster
Sport Sedan (4-door)
Town Sedan (2-door)
Club Coupe
Business Coupe

Their recurrent advertising theme "Chevrolet is Number One" again appears in this 1948 advertisement.

1948 "T-bar" grill trim

Little apparent change occurred in 1948, the last year for the warmed-over pre-war styling. A new grill treatment added some visual difference by bolting a vertical "T-bar" over the 1947 grill.

The distinctions between the Stylemaster and Fleetmaster series were continued with the former furnished with a three-spoke plain steering wheel and painted dashboard on which some dress-up trim is omitted. The clock, cigarette lighter, and light in the package compartment remained standard on the Fleetmaster series only.

The Fleetline Aerosedan and its companion four-door, the Sportmaster Sedan, continued to be considered as a part of the Fleetmaster series, and do not have a separate Series designation.

S P E C I F I C A T I O N S

ENGINE: Six cylinders, valve-in-head. Specialized 4-way oiling system, combining pressure streams to connecting rods (instant cold-starting lubrication) and positive feed to crankshaft, camshaft, and valve rocker-arms. Single-adjustment downdraft carburetor with air cleaner, silencer, and flame arrester; automatic fuel-mixture heater, with thermostatic control; 16-gallon fuel tank. Permanently lubricated leakproof water pump, self-adjusting; individual cylinder cooling, with full-length water jackets; nozzle-jet cooling of valve seats; coolant capacity, 15 quarts. Delco-Remy ignition, with centrifugal and vacuum spark-advance control, and octane selector; waterproof coil; high-output generator, with voltage and current regulator; mechanical-shift starter. Diaphragm-spring clutch; permanently lubricated ball throw-out bearing. Syncro-Mesh transmission, helical gears throughout; vacuum-power gearshift. Counterbalanced crankshaft, with precision interchangeable main bearings and rubber-floated harmonic balancer. Pistons of lightweight cast alloy iron, surface-treated. Power plant mounted on three-point rubber-cushioned support, with two rubber torque-reaction dampers.

CHASSIS: Box-girder frame. Unitized Knee-Action front suspension, with fully sealed bearings; ride stabilizer. Semi-elliptic rear springs, rubber insulated; metal spring covers. Double-acting hydraulic shock absorbers, front and rear. Fully enclosed universal joint and propeller shaft. Semi-floating rear axle, hypoid gears; ratio, 4.11 to 1. Fully adjustable (worm and ball-bearing roller sector) steering gear; shockproof steering; ratio 17½ to 1. Hydraulic brakes; 11-inch drums, self-aligning full-contact brake shoes. Five steel disc wheels, five 6.00-16 tires. (Special extra-low pressure tires on wide-rim 15-inch wheels, optional at extra cost. White sidewall tires, either standard or optional size, at extra cost.) Wheelbase, 116 inches. Over-all length, including bumpers, 197¾ inches (Station Wagon, 207½ inches). Bumper with two guards, front and rear (bumperettes with guards at rear of Station Wagon). Splash and gravel deflectors, front and rear (except rear of Station Wagon).

ELECTRICAL: Sealed Beam headlamps, with foot-controlled switch; beam indicator on speedometer dial. Parking lamps mounted in radiator grille. Two tail and stop lights (one on Station Wagon). Rear license-plate light. Dome light; automatic switch at driver's door on Fleetline and Fleetmaster. Illuminated ignition lock. Adjustable (bright to dim) indirect instrument lighting. Lighting switch with 30-ampere thermal circuit breaker. Dual matched horns. Fifteen-plate 100-ampere-hour battery.

ALL BODIES: No Draft ventilation. Concealed entrance steps with safety treads. Concealed door hinges. Stainless steel moldings on body crease line, and on lower edge of body. Foot scraper at each front door.

SEDANS AND COUPES: Fisher Unisteel construction, with Turret Top and solid steel underbody. Safety plate glass throughout. Bright-finished metal moldings framing windshield and windows of Fleetmaster and Fleetline bodies; decorative moldings on Fleetline fenders. Three-passenger adjustable front seat, full-width cushion (divided back in two-door sedans and coupes). Provision for heater installation under front seat. Pile fabric upholstery in Stylemaster and Fleetmaster bodies; two-tone Bedford cord optional in Fleetmaster bodies; high-quality broadcloth in Fleetline bodies. Leatherette scuff coverings on doors and front seats (also on rear seats of Fleetmaster and Fleetline). Carpet inserts in front-floor rubber mat (except Stylemaster). Two leather-topped front seat arm rests in Fleetmaster and Fleetline. Large illuminated luggage compartment (two in Business Coupe). Key lock at each front door and for trunk.

CHEVROLET
THE ONLY CAR IN THE LOW-PRICE FIELD THAT HAS
BODY BY FISHER

BODY BY FISHER

The entire body structure and each of its doors are all-steel units of Unisteel construction, assuring the highest degree of solidity, durability and safety. The body shell is made up of the floor, Turret Top, cowl and body panels, skillfully reinforced and welded together to form an all-steel structure of extraordinary strength. Note the all-steel welded doors, with solid inner and outer panels—a construction that enables Chevrolet to invite a comparative door-slam test.

1948 Fleetline Aerosedan

1948 Fleetmaster Sport Sedan

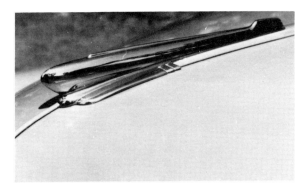

A restyled hood ornament appears for 1948.

1948 Stylemaster Town Sedan

Andy Keksis, San Diego, California

The 1948 hood emblem is similar to the 1947 style (page 44), but they are not identical.

The appearance of the grill is greatly changed by the addition of the vertical trim at its center.

The added "T-bar" front grill trim is prominently embossed at its upper end.

This is the last year for the painted headlight bezel which has been unchanged since 1942.

The bumper tips are accessories added as much to improve the appearance as to protect the fenders.

Rectangular parking lights are concealed at the grill ends.

1948 front view

1947 front view

These front bumper guards are standard on all models.

This is an accessory bumper "tip", designed to give more massive appearance to the bumpers.

1948

The Stylemaster line (right) continues to share the same body shell with the Fleetmaster Series. Its front fenders are, like the Fleetmasters, unadorned except for the lower trim strip (below right). Only the two Fleetline sedans are provided with the additional three fender stripes (below left).

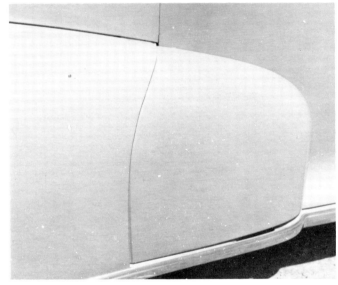

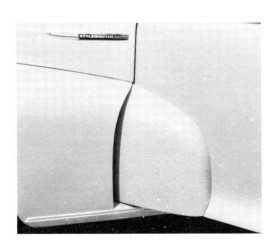

Standard tire size for 1948 is 6:00 x 16, with whitewalls offered at extra cost. Another option was introduced in 1948, the low-pressure 15" tire and wheel.

Although the glass is the same, the bright metal trim used around the windshield of the Fleetmaster series (right) is omitted on the lower priced Stylemaster (above).

The separate door lock located under the handle is used for the last time.

The radio antenna continues to be mounted on the left side of the cowl when the accessory radio is installed.

The Fleetline Aerosedan (above), with its smoothly flowing rear roof line, sharply differs in this area with the Town Sedan (right) although both are two-door sedans.

The top-of-the-line Fleetline Aerosedan not only has the three stripes on its rear fender matching those on the front, but also bears four vertical trim stripes at the rear below the tail lights. These trim sets are not used on the Stylemaster series cars (right).

Inside door locks are provided with knobs which protrude through the window sills.

Rubber gravel guards are provided on all models. These are chromed dress-up accessories, as are the chromed wheel rings.

These are accessory rear bumper tips which match those used on the front (page 61).

Two standard bumper guards are used on the rear bumpers of all models.

All models except the Station Wagon which is bare, and the two Fleetline sedans (below) bear the Chevrolet script on their rear deck lid.

The closed lid is secured with this latch, operated by an external handle (left).

A simplified trunk locking handle appeared in 1947 and is continued on the 1948 models. (compare page 37).

A spacious luggage compartment is found in the Stylemaster Town Sedan. Note that the rear window, like the windshield, is not bright-metal framed on Stylemaster cars.

The instrument panel of the Stylemaster series cars is less elaborate than that of Fleetmasters. Paint replaces the wood-grained finish and dress-up trim is omitted.

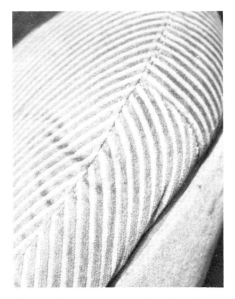

The upholstery used in the Stylemaster differs from that found in Fleetmaster cars.

The Stylemaster series cars are not furnished with a horn-blowing ring on the steering wheel, and the horn button differs (page 52).

Stylemaster cars are provided with three-spoke steering wheels; the turn signals are an accessory.

The 1948 Stylemaster Town Sedan instrument panel

This knob on the instrument panel operates the windshield wipers.

An ash receptacle is furnished in all cars.

The radio is unchanged from 1947.

The Stylemaster series cars have less dress-up trim surrounding their instruments than do the Fleetmasters (page 54), hence the difference in their appearance.

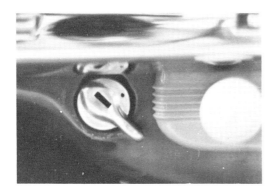

A new ignition switch, introduced on 1948 models, incorporates a bat handle for easier operation. Stylemaster Throttle and Choke (right) knobs are lettered for function.

The two-door Town Sedan has a comfortable bench type
rear seat, and divided front seat.

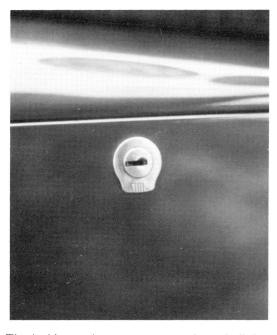

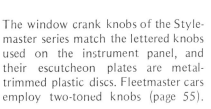

The window crank knobs of the Stylemaster series match the lettered knobs
used on the instrument panel, and
their escutcheon plates are metal-
trimmed plastic discs. Fleetmaster cars
employ two-toned knobs (page 55).

The locking package compartment has a built-in
light on the Fleetmaster models only.

The hood opens from the front for access to the engine compartment.

A shroud is provided to duct the incoming air through the radiator for maximum cooling effect. The cable-operated hood release latch also has a mechanical safety hook, mounted to the hood, which engages its forward lip.

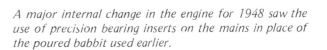

A major internal change in the engine for 1948 saw the use of precision bearing inserts on the mains in place of the poured babbit used earlier.

The distributor is located on the right side of the block.

The coil continues to be mounted on the block above the disbributor. During 1948 the polarity reversing switch introduced on the distributor in 1941 to prolong point life was eliminated.

The external oil filter bolted to the manifold is an accessory.

1949

Series GK   DE LUXE
       Fleetline 4-door Sedan
       Fleetline 2-door Sedan
       Styleline 4-door Sedan
       Styleline 2-door Sedan
       Styleline Sport Coupe
       Styleline Convertible
       Styleline Station Wagon

Series GJ   SPECIAL
       Fleetline 4-door Sedan
       Fleetline 2-door Sedan
       Styleline 4-door Sedan
       Styleline 2-door Sedan
       Styleline Sport Coupe
       Styleline Business Coupe

In an unusual approach to the nation's farmers, Chevrolet extolled "the most beautiful BUY of all" in *Country Magazine* early in 1949.

The eagerly awaited initial post-war design appeared at last, and for 1949, Chevrolet had whipped up a few surprises. Both the earlier Fleetmaster and Stylemaster series names were gone, to be replaced by De Luxe Series and Special series respectively. In each of the two, there was to be found both a Fleetline (fastback) and a Styleline (bustle back) four door and two door sedan.

The new cars were built on a 115" wheelbase, one inch shorter than 1948, but with their newly styled flowing lines they appeared longer and lower. Front fender lines were eliminated, although the rear fenders remained obvious. Smaller 15" wheels were used to lower the car slightly, and a new "center-point" steering which changed the geometry of the steering control was introduced along with a revised Knee Action and airplane-type tubular shock absorbers.

The new De Luxe Series was provided with a nameplate on the front fenders. The Special Series had no similar identification.

SPECIFICATIONS

POWER PLANT

Engine Type: Valve-in-Head, 90 horsepower. Six cylinders, 6.6:1 compression ratio.

Pistons: Lightweight, cast alloy iron, with slipper skirt, surface treated.

Crankshaft: Four, precision interchangeable, thin wall babbitt main bearings. Counterbalanced. Rubber floated harmonic balancer.

Oiling System: Specialized system with pressure streams of oil to the connecting rod bearings, instant cold starting lubrication, and positive pressure to crankshaft bearings, camshaft bearings, valve rocker arms and timing gear spray nozzle.

Fuel System: Single-adjustment balanced downdraft carburetor, with accelerating pump. Octane Selector. A.C. air cleaner, silencer and flame arrester. Fuel mixture heated (thermostatic control) in manifold heat-chamber.

Cooling System: Capacity, 16 quarts. Self-adjusting, permanently lubricated water pump. Individually cooled cylinders, full length water jackets. Nozzle jet valve seat cooling.

Electrical System: Delco-Remy ignition with centrifugal and vacuum spark-advance control. High intensity spark for heavy duty ignition. High output ventilated generator with voltage and current regulator. Delco-Remy starter, with solenoid-operated, positive shift (push button on dash).

Power Plant Mounting: Three point, rubber cushioned support with two shear-type rubber torque reaction dampeners.

Clutch: Diaphragm spring type, ventilated. Permanently lubricated ball throwout bearings.

Transmission: Synchro-mesh with helical gears throughout. Manually operated steering column mounted gearshift control.

CHASSIS

Frame: Box-girder type. In the Convertible a "VK" structure of "I" beam members takes place of Engine Rear Support Cross Member.

Front Suspension: Unitized Knee-action, with fully-adjusting bearings and direct double-acting hydraulic shock absorbers. Ride Stabilizer.

Rear Axle: Semi-floating type with hypoid-drive gears of 4.11 to 1 ratio.

Rear Springs: Semi-elliptic springs and shackles of tension type. Rubber insulated. Metal spring covers. Direct double-acting hydraulic shock absorbers.

Drive System: Torque tube drive. Tubular propeller shaft; both fully enclosed.

Brakes: Four-wheel hydraulic. 11" brake drums.

Self-aligning, full contact brake shoes. Mechanical parking brakes with L-shaped pull handle.

Steering Gear: Ball bearing mounted roller sector; worm mounted on tapered roller bearings; fully adjustable. Ratio 17.4 to 1. Center-point steering. Wheel diameter, 17¼"; all special models, three-spoke with horn button, all de luxe models two-spoke with horn blowing ring.

Wheels and Tires: Five; steel disc with short spokes. 6.70-15 tires on wide base rims. Tire pressure, 24 pounds (Station Wagons 24 pounds front, 30 pounds rear).

Wheelbase: 115 inches. Over-all length 197" (including bumpers). Station Wagon 198" (including bumpers).

Chassis Equipment: Bumpers with two guards, both front and rear. Splash and gravel deflectors front and rear. License guard in front.

LIGHTS—HORN—BATTERY

Lights: Sealed Beam headlamps with foot controlled beam indicator light on instrument panel. Parking lights blended into each side of radiator grille. Dual tail and stop lights on all models except Station Wagons, which have one. Rear license plate lights. Dome light in all models. Dual Matched Horns.

Battery: 15-Plate, 100 ampere-hour capacity.

INSTRUMENT PANEL—CONTROLS—VISION

Instruments: Speedometer. Oil pressure and gasoline gauges. Battery charge and engine heat indicators. Variable indirect instrument cluster lighting.

Controls: Rubber padded foot controls. Illuminated, 3 position ignition lock. Lights, choke, throttle, air intake and windshield wiper controls.

Vision: Single control dual windshield wipers. Two windshield defroster openings. Adjustable inside rear view mirror (outside on Convertible coupe).

BODY EQUIPMENT—SPECIAL MODELS

Regular equipment on Special models includes the following:

Exterior: Dual tail and stop lights. Dual license lights. Dual horns. Dual windshield wipers. Stainless steel body belt line molding. Stainless steel body sill moldings. Stainless steel rear fender crown moldings. Curved windshield with stainless steel center molding. Push-button door handles with key locks in both front doors. Black rubber fender shields. Gasoline filler compartment under door in left rear fender. Hood ornament and emblem. Rear deck lid emblem. Chrome-plated headlight rims. Five extra-low pressure tires, size 6.70-15, on five-inch rims. Bumpers and bumper guards, front and rear. License guard on front bumper.

Interior: Seats upholstered with tan, striped pattern, pile fabric with rubber-sized back. Doors, sidewalls, and ceiling trimmed with fabrics in solid colors to harmonize with seat material. Brown leather fabric scuff pads with stainless steel molding, radio across top, on all doors. Brown leather fabric facing across top of rear seat back. Carpet on rear floors of sedans and Sport Coupe. Business Coupe has black rubber floor mat in front compartment and luggage compartment. Business Coupe has black rubber mat on floor behind front seat. Sunshade for driver. Inside rear view mirror. Three-spoke steering wheel with horn button in center. Circular instrument cluster, including speedometer with glass figure ring, temperature gauge, fuel gauge, ammeter, and oil pressure gauge. Instrument panel includes nameplate, stainless steel horizontal molding, radio grille, glove compartment with lock, and removable panels for installation of accessory radio controls, clock, ash tray, and cigarette lighter. Brown, deep-luster metallic lacquer on instrument panel and garnish moldings. Contrasting Florida Gray stripe on lower edges of garnish moldings. Plastic control knobs for light switch, throttle, choke, windshield wiper, hood release, ventilators, and window regulators. Dual ventilators in dash. Friction-type ventipanes with drip shields in both front doors. Lowering quarter windows in two-door sedans. Lowering forward sections and fixed ventipanes in rear door windows of four-door sedans. Fixed quarter windows in coupes. Robe cord in four-door sedans. Two coat hooks. Dome light with integral switch. "Body by Fisher" emblem on right side of front seat. Painted step plates at door openings. Bumper jack, and combination jack handle and wheel wrench.

BODY EQUIPMENT—DE LUXE MODELS

Regular equipment on De Luxe models includes the following, in addition to, or in place of the regular equipment listed for Special models.

Exterior: Series nameplate (De Luxe) on front fenders. Stainless steel moldings on front fenders and doors. Stainless steel windshield reveal. Stainless steel rear fender shields. Stainless steel side and back window reveals, except on Convertible Coupe and Station Wagons. Short section of belt molding on front doors of Steel Station Wagon. None on Wood Station Wagon. Rear wheel cover panels. Outside rear view mirror on left front door of Convertible Coupe (in place of inside mirror).

Interior, Sedans and Sport Coupe: Seats upholstered with tan, striped pattern, flat cloth. Tan, striped pattern, free-breathing, pile fabric optional. Foam

rubber seat pads. Doors and sidewalls trimmed in two-tone combination of tan and brown solid color fabrics, separated by stainless steel molding. Scuff pads on quarter panels of two-door sedans and Sport Coupe. Tan rubber floor mat in front compartment and luggage compartment. Simulated carpet inserts in front floor mat. Two sunshades. Two-spoke steering wheel with horn-blowing ring. Lucite figure ring on speedometer face. Instrument panel includes automatic glove box light, clock, ash tray, and cigarette lighter. Two-tone instrument panel finish of tan and brown deep-luster metallic lacquer. Garnish moldings painted to match tan area of instrument panel. Stainless steel molding across bottom of each garnish molding. Stainless steel inserts in ivory plastic control knobs for light switch, choke, throttle, windshield wiper, and window regulators. Friction-type ventipanes in rear doors of four-door sedans. Fixed quarter windows in Sport Coupe. Robe cord. Automatic dome light switch in each front door. Arm rests on doors, front and rear, and on quarter panels of two-door sedans and Sport Coupe. Assist straps in two-door sedans and Sport Coupe. Ash trays in front seat back of four-door sedans. Ash trays in arm rests of two-door sedans and Sport Coupe. Extra roof insulation. Molding between rear seat back and package shelf painted brown. Etched aluminum step plates at door openings with "Body by Fisher" emblem on front seat plates. (None at front seat.)

Interior, Convertible Coupe: Equipment similar to other models except:

Seats upholstered with combination of genuine leather and tan Bedford cord. Doors trimmed with leather fabric and tan Bedford cord. Sidewalls, seat back, and sunshades trimmed in leather fabric to match leather on seats. Genuine carpet inserts in front floor mat. Instrument panel and garnish moldings painted body color. Ash trays and arm rests in rear quarter panels. Dome light on roof bow with switch in left quarter panel. No coat hooks, robe cord, or drip shields.

Interior, Station Wagons: Equipment similar to other models except:

Tan leather fabric on seats, sunshades, and scuff pads. Foam rubber seat pad on front seat only. Ceiling trimmed with wood-grained leather fabric. Wood panels on doors and sidewalls (no stainless steel molding). Garnish moldings finished with wood grain. Tan rubber floor mat between front and intermediate seat. Tan linoleum on floor below and behind intermediate seat. Plain ivory knobs on window regulators. Sliding quarter windows. No rear seat arm rests, coat hooks, assist straps, robe cord, or extra roof insulation.

1949

1949 De Luxe Styleline 2-door Sedan

1949 De Luxe Styleline Sport Coupe

The early 1949 literature offered both the all-wood body and the new metal bodied station wagon. However, quite early in the model year the all-wood body was phased out of production in favor of the newer model.

1949 De Luxe Station Wagon

Sun visor and Sportlight are accessories.

1949

The appearance of the 1949 model is greatly changed by both the use of a new grill, a wider and lower hood, and a built-in license plate frame in the front bumper.

A new hood ornament appears.

Resembling the hood insignia first used in 1947, the 1949 unit differs somewhat, having a scribed decor added behind the Chevrolet bow tie.

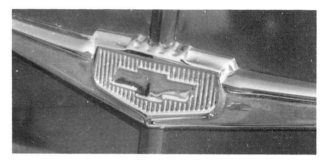

C-H-E-V-R-O-L-E-T is embossed on the top grill bar.

Bumper guards are standard on all models.

The headlamp doors are again chromed, a feature not seen since 1941.

Parking lights are built into the grill.

Wheels are now 15", slightly lowering the cars. Standard tires are low-pressure 6:70 x 15 blackwalls, and the hub caps have red centers. Above the wheelhousing opening is a narrow body stripe trim which is a feature used on the De Luxe series only.

The conspicuous short vertical struts between the two lower bars of the grill are a salient feature of the 1949 model and help to identify it quickly.

A new two-piece curved windshield appears in 1949. The bright metal trim around it is used only on the De Luxe series, and only a rubber moulding is seen on the Standard.

A new vent window latch is used for the first time.

When appropriate, the De Luxe insignia is located on the sides just ahead of the front doors.

The stainless steel beltline moulding is used on both Series.

A new outside door handle with an integral keylock eliminates the separate lock as previously used.

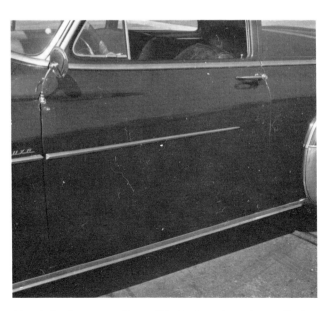

Front fenders, as a discernible feature, have been eliminated by smoothly fairing them into the wider body.

This is the rear quarter of the Styleline body which drops sharply to the bustle-like luggage compartment. The roofline of the Fleetline design slopes gently to the rear bumper (page 65).

Stainless steel rear fender crown mouldings are used on both Special and De Luxe models.

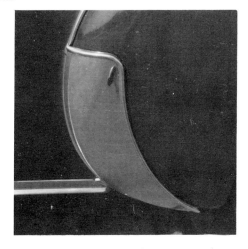

The rear fender shields (gravel guards) are stainless steel on the De Luxe cars, black rubber on the Specials.

The customary rain gutter is provided above the windows.

Rear wheel cover panels are standard on the De Luxe series and are supported from hangers attached to the fenders.

The Fuel filler cap is now located under a flap on the left rear fender. Surrounding the tube is an apron to block spilled fuel.

The stainless steel trim at the rear window is used only on the De Luxe series cars.

A surprisingly large luggage compartment is found beneath the rear deck of the 2-door sedans. By relocating the spare wheel additional storage volume is obtained. A rubber mat protects the floor of the compartment, and its interior is lighted by a window in each tail light.

NEW EXCITING

... MUSTANG Does It!
... NIFTY FIFTIES Fords
... The Real CORVETTE
... THUNDERBIRD!
... HENRY'S LADY
... V/8 AFFAIR

FULL CO OR POSTERS

- 23" x 36" full color wall posters depicting exciting model years.
- Printed on high gloss, attractive, poster stock, suitable for framing or free hanging.
- Many different models and years displayed in vivid color.
- Shipped rolled, in sturdy protective cardboard tubes.

$3.95 each
POST PAID

ORDER NOW FOR IMMEDIATE DELIVERY!

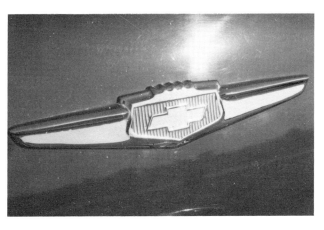

A duplicate of the insignia on the hood appears also on the rear deck lid.

New vertical tail lights, incorporating a flat lens, appear in 1949.

A locking T-handle is used, but couriously, the handle does not turn. Rotating the key opens the latch.

New lights are placed on either side of the rear license plate to illuminate it.

The rear bumper, like that in front, is furnished with two guards and wraps around the fender for added protection. The backup light is an accessory.

1949   *Early in the 1949 model year, Chevrolet's literature offered both the "Natural Wood Body" Station Wagon, and also another with all-steel body. Both were listed as Styleline De Luxe Station Wagons, and both were illustrated, although the newer all-steel model appeared more prominently.*

In addition to the obvious difference in the construction of the body, the all-steel Station Wagon was designed to seat eight passengers and included a rear (third) seat which was not provided in the wooden body. It also was given a modest additional stainless steel trim at the base of its windshield which wrapped around onto the front doors, but otherwise rese[mbled] the earlier, and obsolescent wood bodied version.

The wooden bodied station wagon was obviously a com[pro]mise since, unlike the 1948 version, it now had an all-st[eel] roof in place of the earlier batten-and-fabric top, and [was] destined to see limited production. Early in the year it [was] discontinued in favor of the all-steel model and now ra[nks] among the rarest of the early post-war Chevrolets.

1949 De Luxe Station Wagon (wood body version)

1949 De Luxe Station Wagon
all-steel body

This car has several accessories. Many are noted on the following page.

Mr. John Hunt, San Diego, California

1949

This well-restored feature car has been provided with many accessories. Several are given special mention here to avoid possible misunderstanding as to originality.

An external sun visor is installed over the windshield.

A red-plastic tipped dress-up hood ornament replaces the standard 1949 item (page 76).

A grill guard adds frontal protection.

Accessory driving lamps are affixed to the lower grill bar.

Not only one, but *dual* spotlights are installed. Control for each is inside the car by means of a pistol-type grip.

A relatively small portion of the "natural wood" bodied Station Wagon is actually constructed of the material.

The door handle is similar to, but not interchangeable with, the new passenger car locking handles. Locks are provided on the front door handles only.

The doors are both hinged at their forward edge for easy entry.

A nameplate on the left front door pillar shows the serial number of the car.

The quarter windows are of the sliding type; those in the doors can be lowered.

1949

Starting with the 1949 models, Chevrolet ingeniously stored the spare wheel and tire under the floor of the rear deck which is hinged at its forward edge to allow access. The use of dual matching tail lights on this car suggest the installation of accessory turn signals.

The lift gate can be latched in its open position.

A T-handle on the lift gate contains a keylock. Unlike the similar unit on the sedans, this one *is* rotated to release the latch.

The 1949 winged insignia appears on the tail gate.

Headliner material is a wood-grained leather fabric, and the metal bows are also wood-grained for best effect.

The headlining of the Station Wagon is installed over a set of visible bows and under the solid steel roof panel.

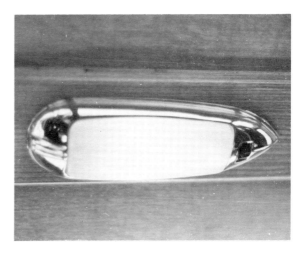

A dome light, similar to that used in the Special sedans, with an integral switch, is used in the Station Wagons. De Luxe cars also have automatic switches in the front doors.

The tail lights used on the Station Wagons are hinged to maintain the lens in the vertical position even when the tail gate is lowered. Normally only one light is furnished, in the center of the tailgate, but a matching unit is generally installed with accessory turn signals.

The hub of the De Luxe steering wheel is decorated with the bow tie insignia in a red background matching the decoration on the hub caps.

De Luxe cars are furnished with a two-spoke steering wheel with a unique half-circle horn blowing ring. Special series cars have a three-spoke wheel with no horn ring.

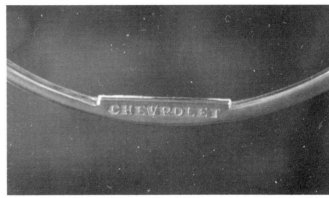

The Chevrolet name appears on the horn ring.

Instruments are re-grouped into a circular assembly and placed directly in front of the driver where they can be viewed through the circle of the steering wheel. Flanking this assembly are appropriate control knobs.

Knobs on the dashboard controls are plain ivory plastic on the Specials, but those on the De Luxe have a stainless steel insert as seen here. The push button above the Throttle knob is the starter control, new this year, replacing the former foot-operated switch.

A Chevrolet script is affixed to the center of the instrument panel which is painted brown in the Special Series and two-toned in tan-and-brown in the De Luxe.

The integrated instrument cluster in the De Luxe, shown here, is provided with a lettered Lucite bezel. On the Special cars, this is made of glass.

The instrument panel clock, the ash tray beneath it, and the cigarette lighter below that, are all accessories in the Special Series, but are standard in the De Luxe.

The accessory radio has been restyled and now has an easier-to-read tuning dial.

Featured as "the car that 'Breathes' for all-weather comfort", a new ventilating system provides standard dual intake vents at the front of the car to bring fresh air in. These vents are controlled by two knobs suspended beneath the dashboard.

The "Lumidor" knob suspended under the dashboard is the control for the accessory driving lights shown on page 84. The upper knob is the headlight switch.

Early in 1949, the hood release was cable-operated with a knob under the dashboard. During the year, however, this mechanism was discarded and a release latch provided at the front.

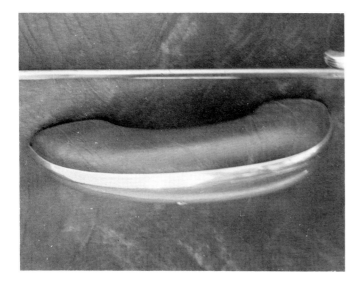

Arm rests are provided on the De Luxe series, and the upholstery of the closed cars is trimmed with a stainless steel garnish moulding (above). The door panels of the Station Wagon are of wood (right).

The door handles and window regulators of the Station Wagon and Standard Series resemble the style used earlier, but the window crank knobs match those on the instrument panel. Note the separate escutcheon plates.

The door handles and window cranks of the other De Luxe Series cars have an integral "skirt" and the crank knobs, like those on the instrument panel, have a stainless steel insert.

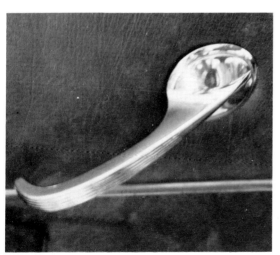

This new, flatter, air cleaner made its appearance in 1949 to accommodate the somewhat flatter and lower hood.

NEW CHEVROLET *for* 1950

Smarter Styling · New Luxuries · Improved Performance

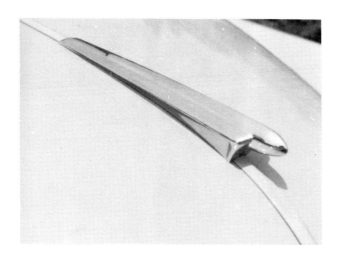

Series HK   DE LUXE

    Bel Air
    Fleetline 2-door Sedan
    Fleetline 4-door Sedan
    Styleline 2-door Sedan
    Styleline 4-door Sedan
    Styleline Sport Coupe
    Styleline Convertible
    Styleline Station Wagon

Series HJ   SPECIAL

    Fleetline 2-door Sedan
    Fleetline 4-door Sedan
    Styleline 2-door Sedan
    Styleline 4-door Sedan
    Styleline Sport Coupe
    Styleline Business Coupe

Generally similar to the 1949 style, Chevrolet's 1950 models had but few changes. A new grill, hood and trunk lid ornamentation, and some minor trim changes were all that marked the difference, for the major styling change provided in 1949 had yet to saturate its market.

In addition to all of the models produced in 1949 (except for the "natural wood body" Station Wagon), Chevrolet scored a real coup with its introduction of the first "hardtop Convertible", the Bel Air. With its disappearing side posts which lowered with the windows, and its broad wrap-around rear window, the car was an immediate success. The Bel Air was to inspire a similar model by competitors (Ford and Plymouth brought out models in 1951), and also was to lend its name to an entire series of top-of-the-line Chevrolets.

Although higher-priced cars, including GM's own Cadillac, had offered such an option for almost ten years, no low-priced car had provided it until Chevrolet, during 1950, introduced its now-famous Powerglide automatic transmission accessory on the De Luxe models. Featuring a Low and Drive forward selection in addition to Reverse, Neutral, and a gear-locking Park position, the unit was a fairly smooth operating accessory that was eagerly ordered, especially in the top of the line cars.

Chevrolet continued its proven six cylinder engine, now with a new Rochester carburetor in all cars, however, those equipped with Powerglide were provided with a modified version of the truck engine which had a 1/16" larger bore (3-9/16") and a 3/16" longer stroke (3-15/16") for the added power necessary to operate the transmission. With the Powerglide-equipped models, a slightly lower ratio rear end (3.55:1) was used.

SPECIFICATIONS

POWER PLANT

gine Type: Valve-in-Head. 92 horsepower. Six inders, 6.6:1 compression ratio, 3½" bore, 3¾" stroke.

stons: Lightweight, cast alloy iron, with slipper skirt, face treated.

ankshaft: Counterbalanced. Four, precision inter-ngeable, thin wall babbitt main bearings. Rubber ated harmonic balancer.

ling System: Specialized system with pressure streams oil to the connecting rod bearings (instant cold starting rication) and positive pressure to crankshaft bearings, nshaft bearings, valve rocker arms and timing gear ay nozzle.

el System: New, single-adjustment balanced down-ft carburetor, with fast-idle mechanism. Octane ector. A.C. air cleaner, silencer and flame arrester. l mixture heated (thermostatic control) in manifold t-chamber. 16-gallon gasoline tank. Fuel tank filler nal (except Station Wagon).

oling System: Capacity, 15 quarts. Self-adjusting, manently lubricated water pump. Individually cooled inders, full length water jackets. Nozzle jet valve seat oling.

ctrical System: Delco-Remy ignition with centrifugal d vacuum spark-advance control. High intensity spark, avy duty ignition. Waterproof coil. High output venti-ed generator with voltage and current regulator. co-Remy starter, with solenoid-operated, positive shift sh button on dash).

wer Plant Mounting: Three-point, rubber-cushioned port with two shear-type rubber torque reaction npeners.

tch: Diaphragm spring type, ventilated. Permanently ricated ball throwout bearing.

nsmission: Synchro-mesh with helical gears through-. Steering column mounted gearshift control.

CHASSIS

me: Box-girder type, reinforced for Bel Air. In the nvertible a "VK" structure of "I" beam members takes ce of engine rear support cross member.

ont Suspension: Unitized Knee-Action, with fully-led bearings and direct double-acting hydraulic shock sorbers. Ride stabilizer.

ar Axle: Semi-floating type with hypoid drive gears 4.11 to 1 ratio.

ar Springs: Semi-elliptic springs and shackles of sion type. Rubber insulated. Metal spring covers. Direct uble-acting hydraulic shock absorbers.

ve System: Torque tube drive. Tubular propeller ft; fully enclosed.

akes: Four-wheel hydraulic. 11" brake drums. Self-aligning, full contact brake shoes. Mechanical parking brakes with L-shaped pull handle.

Steering Gear: Ball bearing mounted roller sector; worm mounted on tapered roller bearings; fully adjustable. Ratio 17.4 to 1. Center-point steering. Wheel diameter, 17¼"; all special models, three-spoke with horn button, all de luxe models two-spoke with horn blowing ring.

Wheels and Tires: Five; steel disc with short spokes. 6.70-15 tires on wide base rims.

Wheelbase: 115 inches. Over-all length (including bumpers) 197½"; Station Wagons, 198¼".

Chassis Equipment: Bumpers with two guards, both front and rear. Splash and gravel deflectors front and rear. License guard in front.

LIGHTS—HORN—BATTERY

Lights: Sealed Beam headlamps with foot controlled beam; indicator light on instrument panel. New, parking lights blended into each side of radiator grille. New, dual tail and stop lights on all models except Station Wagon, which has one. Rear license plate lights. Dome light all models. Dual matched horns.

Battery: 15-Plate, 100 ampere-hour capacity.

INSTRUMENT PANEL—CONTROLS—VISION

Instruments: Speedometer. Oil pressure and gasoline gauges. Battery charge and engine heat indicators. Variable indirect instrument cluster lighting.

Controls: Rubber padded foot controls. Illuminated, 3-position ignition lock. Lights, choke, throttle, air intake and windshield wiper controls.

Vision: Single control dual windshield wipers. Two windshield defroster openings. Adjustable inside rear view mirror (outside on Convertible coupe).

BODY EQUIPMENT—SPECIAL MODELS

Exterior: Stainless steel body belt line molding, body sill moldings, and rear fender crown moldings. Curved windshield with stainless steel center molding. Push-button door handles. Key locks in both front doors. Black rubber rear fender shields. Gasoline filler under door in left rear fender. Hood ornament and new emblem. New deck lid lock and stationary loop type handle. Chrome-plated headlight rims. Bumpers and new bumper guards, front and rear. Front license guard.

Interior: Seat upholstery is gray-striped modern weave flat cloth. Upper side walls, center pillar, front seat-back and side panels are plain dark gray broadcloth and lower side walls are plain light gray fabric. Headlining is light gray fabric. Seat and side wall two-tone gray combination. Dark gray leather fabric scuff pads with stainless steel molding across top, on all doors. Carpet on rear floors of sedans and Sport Coupe. Black rubber floor mat in front compartment and luggage compartment. Business Coupe has black rubber mat on floor behind front seat. Sunshade for driver. Inside rear view mirror. Circular instrument cluster, including speedometer. Instrument panel includes stainless steel horizontal molding, radio grille, glove compartment with lock, and removable panels for installation of accessory radio controls, clock, ash tray, and cigarette lighter. Dark gray, on instrument panel and garnish moldings. Contrasting light gray stripe on lower edges of garnish moldings. Light gray control knobs for light switch, throttle, choke, windshield wiper, ventilators, and window regulators. Friction-type ventipanes with drip shields in both front doors. Lowering quarter windows in two-door sedans. Lowering forward sections and fixed ventipanes in rear door windows of four-door sedans. Fixed quarter windows in coupes. Two coat hooks. Dome light with integral switch. "Body by Fisher" emblem on right side of front seat. Luggage compartment illuminated from clear glass window in each tail light. Painted step plates at door openings. Bumper jack, and combination jack handle and wheel wrench.

BODY EQUIPMENT—DE LUXE MODELS

Regular equipment on De Luxe models includes the following, in addition to, or in place of the regular equipment listed for Special models:

Exterior, Sedans and Coupes: Stainless steel windshield, door window, quarter window, and rear window reveals. Series nameplate (De Luxe) in chrome, above stainless steel moldings on front fenders and doors. Stainless steel rear fender shields. Rear wheel cover panels.

Exterior, Convertible Coupe: Equipment similar to Sedan and Sport Coupe except: chrome-plated side window frames. Rear window glass enclosed in die cast frame and mounted in fabric zipper-curtain. Outside rear view mirror mounted on left front door, in place of inside mirror. Hydraulically operated folding fabric top.

Exterior, Bel Air Model: Equipment similar to Convertible except: All-steel, stationary top. Enlarged rear window with stainless steel moldings. No outside rear view mirror.

Exterior, Station Wagon: Equipment similar to Sedan models except: Simulated wood grained steel panels. No stainless steel window reveal moldings. Stainless steel body belt molding extends across base of windshield and on front doors to rear edge of ventipanes. Gasoline filler cap on left rear fender.

Interior, Sedans and Sport Coupe: Foam rubber seat cushion pads. Seat upholstery is gray, striped, broadcloth with shoulder area of seat back cushion of plain dark gray broadcloth. The rear face of the front seat back cushion, the seat riser, upper side walls, and center pillar are also dark gray broadcloth. Light gray lower side walls, and a harmonizing light gray headlining. Scuff pads on all doors, and quarter panels of two-door sedans and sport coupe are of dark gray leather fabric. Dark gray rubber floor mat in front compartment and tan rubber in luggage compartment. Simulated carpet inserts of gray flecked rubber in front floor mat. Harmonizing gray, deep pile carpet on rear seat floor area. Two sunshades. Circular instrument cluster with Lucite face. Instrument panel includes radio grille, glove compartment with lock and automatic light, clock, ash tray, cigarette lighter, and removable panel for installation of accessory radio controls. Stainless steel inserts in dark gray plastic control knobs for light switch, choke, throttle, windshield wiper and window regulators. Light gray plastic knobs for selector lever and ventilator controls. Friction type ventipanes in rear doors of four-door sedans. Sliding quarter windows in Sport Coupe. Robe cord. Automatic dome light switch in each front door. Arm rest on doors, front and rear, and on quarter panels of two-door sedans and Sport Coupe. Assist straps in two-door sedans and Sport Coupe. Ash tray in front seat-back of four-door sedans, and one in each rear seat armrest in two-door sedans and Sport Coupe. Extra roof insulation.

Interior, Convertible Coupe: Equipment similar to Sedan and Sport Coupe models except:

Seats upholstered in a combination of genuine leather and two-tone gray, striped, pile cord fabric. Doors and side-walls trimmed in leather fabric and two-tone gray, striped, pile cord fabric. Front seat back, and sunshades trimmed in leather fabric to match leather on seats. Genuine carpet inserts in front floor mat and genuine carpet on rear seat floor area. Upper part of instrument panel and garnish moldings painted leather trim color. Steering wheel rim, outer ends of spokes, and hub around medallion colored black, other painted parts light gray. Ash trays and arm rests in rear quarter panels. Dome light on roof bow with manual switch in left rear quarter panel. No coat hooks, robe cord, or drip shields. Interior-Exterior Color Combinations: Two-tone gray, striped, pile cord fabric is the same for all color combinations of this model. Colors of fabric top, top boot, seat and side wall leather trim, garnish moldings, and upper part of instrument panel change with body color.

Interior, Bel Air: Same as Convertible Coupe except:

Rear compartment lights—two, 6 candlepower each; one in each roof quarter panel just above belt line. Headlining—neutral gray fabric, exposed bright metal roof bows. Transmission control lever knob, black plastic. Luggage compartment same in size as Sport Coupe.

Interior, Station Wagon: Wood grained garnish moldings, mahogany door panels; seat upholstery and headlining to match. Foam rubber front seat pad.

1950 Bel Air

Chevrolet is still "First" in this ad from Life magazine in early 1950.

1950 Fleetline Special 2-door Sedan

Mr. Elmer Ryan, Bellflower, California

A return to the one-piece bumper sees the elimination of a recessed front license plate frame as used in 1949.

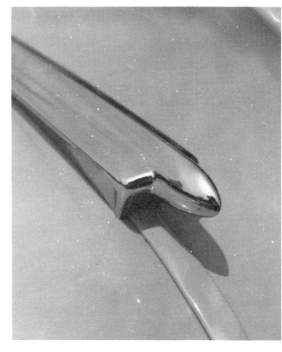

A restyled hood ornament for 1950 eliminates the dorsal fin of the previous model (page 76).

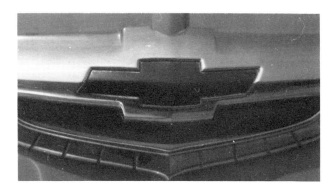

The Chevrolet name continues on the upper grill bar, but a restyled winged insignia appears in 1950 (compare page 76).

The grill takes on a new look with the elimination of five of the seven vertical struts that were used between the two lower bars in 1949. The bumper guards, both front and rear, are standard on all models.

The chromed headlight bezel remains unchanged.

The Chevrolet name is continued on the upper grill bar.

Parking lights, as in 1949, are round, and placed at the ends of the upper grill bar.

The rectangular opening is an intake scoop for Chevrolet's forced air ventilation system. A similar intake is placed at the left side.

The wrap around single piece front bumper is unchanged. Wheels remain at 15", and black-wall 6.70 x 15 tires are standard, and the hub caps now have gold centers.

A stainless steel moulding circles the car at its beltline. Below it is seen the radio antenna which is placed on the left front fender when that accessory is installed.

The curved windshield, its halves separated by a stainless steel trim, continues.

Special Series cars have no stainless trim around the windshield panes, and the black rubber gasket is evident. This gasket differs slightly on the De Luxe cars having an extra slit into which the stainless steel is inserted.

Emphasized in this view, the front fender was incorporated into the body in 1949, and no longer is a discernible entity.

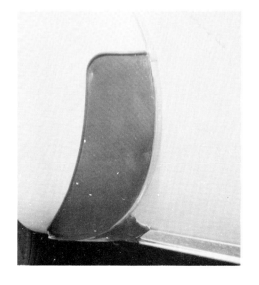

Black rubber rear fender shields are used on the Standard cars. On the De Luxe, these are made of stainless steel.

The rear window of the Special, like its windshield, is not supplied with the bright metal trim which appears on De Luxe series cars.

Doors of the Special Series cars do not have the stripe which leads to the front fender on the De Luxe cars (page 78).

The lines of the rear fenders remain identifiable on all models. The rear quarter of the Fleetline sedans slopes smoothly from roof to bumper, Styleline cars have a definite interruption (page 79).

The rear windows of the Fleetline 2-door sedans can be lowered for ventilation. The 4-doors have rotating ventipanes in their rear doors.

The appearance of the 1950 model differs from that of the 1949 (page 80) due to a restyled deck lid handle (next page).

A new three-dimensional tail light lens replaces the flat style used in 1949 (page 81).

In the 1950 models, the apron around the filler tube (page 79) has been opened up to allow spilled fuel to escape.

The rear gravel shield between the body and the bumper continues to be furnished on all models.

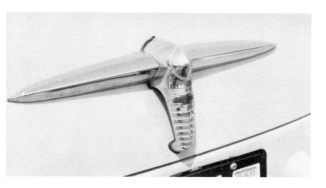

A new rear deck lid trim appears in 1950. The "arms" of this T-shaped insignia bear the word "Powerglide" on cars that are so-equipped.

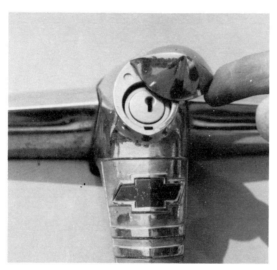

The keylock is concealed by a spring-loaded cap. Turning the key releases the latch; it is not possible to rotate the decorative handle.

A new curve of the cross section of the bumpers requires a redesign of the bumper guards, both front and rear. Two guards are standard on each bumper on all models.

The rear license plate lights introduced in 1949 are continued on the 1950 models.

The Special Series continues to use a three-spoke steering wheel, and its horn button (there is no horn ring) is fairly plain, but does bear bow tie insignia.

The instrument panel in the Special Series contains removable blanking plates for the accessory radio controls, clock, ash tray, and cigarette lighter (De Luxe Series has only accessory radio blanking panel; the other items are standard), and both are trimmed in gray paint and stainless steel.

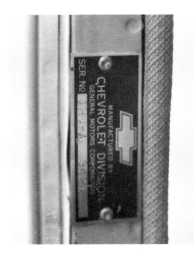

The Chevrolet serial number identification plate continues to be mounted on the left front door jamb.

All models but the Convertible are supplied with an inside rear view mirror. The Convertible has a standard outside mirror mounted on the left front door in place of it.

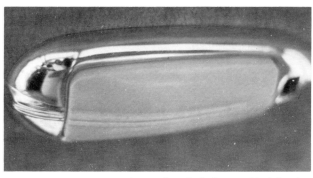

A dome light with an integral switch is provided in the Special Series cars. De Luxe Series cars have automatic switches in the front door posts to turn on light when the door is opened.

Gray is the featured color for the 1950 cars and both Special and De Luxe are upholstered in complimentary fabrics.

The 2-door Sedans have divided front seats to allow access to the rear.

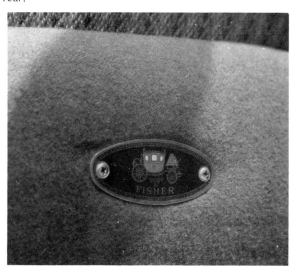

The Fisher Body oval nameplate appears on the front seat platform.

The knobs on the instrument panel and the window cranks are gray plastic in the Special Series. Those in the De Luxe cars are gray with a stainless steel insert like the similar tan knobs used in 1949 (page 91).

The starter motor pushbutton remains on the instrument panel just above the Throttle control knob.

The instrument cluster is unchanged except for color; in 1950 the tint is gray rather than tan.

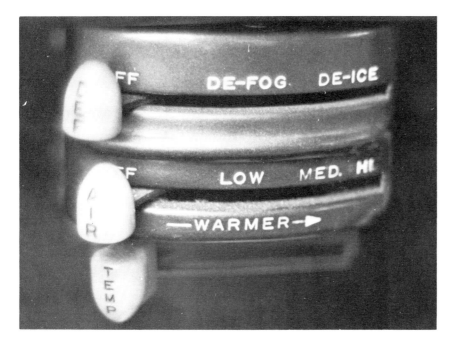

The heater is an accessory, and when installed, its control head is mounted under the instrument panel on the left side where it can be reached by the driver.

Light gray plastic knobs are used on the vent controls in both series.

The Chevrolet script continues to appear on the instrument panel top center. Below it is the standard grill for the accessory radio.

A clock is standard in the De Luxe series, an accessory in the Special.

A locking glove compartment is standard in all models. An interior light is supplied in the De Luxe series cars only.

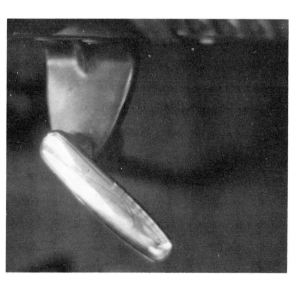

The ash tray and cigarette lighter, like the clock, are accessories in the Special Series cars and if not ordered each of the three openings is covered with a blanking panel.

New in 1950 is this L-shaped handle on the parking brake, now located to the right of the steering wheel, replacing the earlier pistol-grip handle at the far left.

Chevrolet's new Bel Air was an advanced design and inspired similar models in the line of virtually every other domestic automobile manufacturer. Initially, the Bel Air was exclusively a sporty two door, but with its luxurious design, the car developed a rapid following and its name was to later refer to the entire line of higher-priced Chevrolets.

The two most memorable Chevrolet introductions of 1950 would _have_ to be the Bel Air (later to be come to be known as a "hardtop convertible"), and Powerglide, the first automatic transmission offered in a low priced car.

With its windows raised, the Bel Air features narrow "pillars" which are actually the window frames.

With its windows lowered, the windshield "pillars" have disappeared and occupants have an unobstructed view.

A wide wrap-around rear window is used on the Bel Air exclusively.

The "suggestion" of a Convertible's interior is one of the features of the Bel Air. Accomplished by the use of chromed bows under the headliner, the ceiling is most attractive. Interior lights are placed just above the belt line at the rear base of the roof.

The Bel Air instrument panel, while similar to that of the other models has some differences. The transmission shift lever has a black knob, and, like the Convertible, the steering wheel rim, and the outer part of the spokes, is painted black.

CHEVROLET FOR 1951

Series JK   DE LUXE
       Bel Air
       Fleetline 2-door Sedan
       Fleetline 4-door Sedan
       Styleline 2-door Sedan
       Styleline 4-door Sedan
       Sport Coupe
       Convertible
       Station Wagon

Series JJ   SPECIAL
       Fleetline 2-door Sedan
       Fleetline 4-door Sedan
       Styleline 2-door Sedan
       Styleline 4-door Sedan
       Sport Coupe
       Business Coupe

The 1951 model year was largely unchanged from that of 1950, and the major difference appears to be limited to the new grill treatment. No revision was made in the model line-ups, but a new instrument panel layout and larger "Jumbo-Drum" brakes added to driving comfort.

Chevrolet's sturdy 92 horsepower six cylinder engine continued to be the standard power plant in both Series, and a beefed-up 105 horsepower version which featured hydraulic valve lifters and larger bore and stroke was supplied on those cars incorporating the accessory Powerglide automatic transmission. This option continued to be available only in the De Luxe models.

The exciting new Bel Air, which offered, according to the catalog "the smartness of a convertible and all of the practical advantages of a permanent steel top", remained basically unchanged, as did the rest of the line and was destined to develop into an important segment of Chevrolet's production. Although the Styleline sedans continued in popularity, the Fleetline "fastback" models were growing ponderously obsolescent and would soon be discontinued.

SPECIFICATIONS

POWER PLANT

Engine Type: Valve-in-Head. 92 horsepower. Six cylinders, 6.6:1 compression ratio. Bore 3½; stroke 3¾. Lightweight, cast alloy iron, with slipper skirt, surface treated.

Pistons: Counterbalanced. Four, precision interchangeable, thin wall babbitt main bearings. Rubber floated harmonic balancer.

Crankshaft: Counterbalanced. Four, precision interchangeable, thin wall babbitt main bearings. Rubber floated harmonic balancer.

Oiling System: Specialized system with pressure streams of oil to the connecting rod bearings (instant cold starting lubrication) and positive pressure to crankshaft bearings, camshaft bearings, valve rocker arms and timing gears.

Fuel System: Single-adjustment balanced down-draft carburetor, with fast-idle mechanism. Octane Selector. A.C. air cleaner, silencer and flame arrester. Fuel mixture heated (thermostatic control) in manifold heat-chamber. 16-gallon gasoline tank. Fuel tank filler signal (except Station Wagon).

Cooling System: Capacity, 15 quarts. Self-adjusting, permanently lubricated water pump. Individually cooled cylinders, full length water jackets. Nozzle jet valve seat cooling.

Electrical System: Delco-Remy ignition with centrifugal and vacuum spark-advance control. High intensity spark, heavy-duty ignition. Waterproof coil. High output ventilated generator with voltage and current regulator. Delco-Remy starter, with solenoid-operated, positive shift (push button on dash).

Power Plant Mounting: Three point, rubber-cushioned support with two shear-type rubber torque reaction dampeners.

Clutch: Diaphragm spring type, ventilated. Permanently lubricated ball throwout bearings.

Transmission: Synchro-mesh with helical gears throughout. Steering column mounted gearshift control.

CHASSIS

Frame: Box-girder type, reinforced for Bel Air. In the convertible a "VK" structure of "I" beam members takes place of engine rear support cross member.

Front Suspension: Unitized Knee-Action, with fully-sealed bearings and direct double-acting hydraulic shock absorbers. Ride stabilizer.

Rear Axle: Semi-floating type with hypoid drive gears of 4.11 to 1 ratio.

Rear Springs: Semi-elliptic springs and shackles of suspension type. Rubber insulated. Metal spring covers. Direct double-acting hydraulic shock absorbers.

Drive System: Torque tube drive. Tubular propeller shaft; fully enclosed.

Drive Shaft: Four-wheel hydraulic. 11" brake drums. Self-energizing, full contact brake shoes with bonded linings. Mechanical parking brakes with L-shaped pull handle.

Steering Gear: Ball bearing mounted roller sector; worm mounted on tapered roller bearings; fully adjustable. Ratio 19.4 to 1. Center-point steering. Wheel diameter, 17¼"; all special models, three-spoke with

horn button, all De Luxe models two-spoke with full circle horn blowing ring.

Wheels and Tires: Five; steel disc with short spokes. 6.70-15 tires on wide-base rims.

Wheelbase: 115 inches. Over-all length 197¹³⁄₁₆" (including bumpers); Station Wagons, 197⅞".

Chassis Equipment: Bumpers with two guards, both front and rear. Splash and gravel deflectors front and rear. License guard in front.

LIGHTS—HORN—BATTERY

Lights: Sealed Beam headlamps with foot controlled beam; indicator light on instrument panel. Parking lights blended into each side of radiator grille. Dual tail and stop lights on all models except Station Wagon, which has one. Rear license plate light. Dome light all models. Dual matched horns.

Battery: 15-Plate, 100-ampere-hour capacity.

INSTRUMENT PANEL—CONTROLS—VISION

Instruments: Speedometer, oil pressure and gasoline gauges, battery charge and engine heat indicators arranged in two circular clusters. Variable indirect instrument cluster lighting.

Controls: Rubber padded foot controls. Illuminated, 3-position ignition lock. Lights, choke, starter, air intake and windshield wiper controls.

Vision: Single control dual windshield wipers. Two windshield defroster openings. Adjustable inside rearview mirror (outside on Convertible coupe).

BODY EQUIPMENT—SPECIAL MODELS

Exterior: Stainless steel moldings on body belt and sill. Curved windshield with stainless steel center molding. Safety plate glass throughout. Push button side door handles, with key locks in both front doors. Counterbalanced, automatic-locking deck lid with ornamental handle. Black rubber rear fender shields. Hood emblem and ornament. Chrome-plated headlight rims. Concealed gasoline filler.

Interior: Two-tone gray color combination. Light gray striped pattern cloth seat upholstery. Plain dark gray cloth on upper sidewalls with plain light gray cloth below. Leather fabric scuff pads on doors. Rubber floor mat in front compartment. Carpet on rear compartment floors (rubber mat in Business Coupe). Glove compartment with lock, radio grille, and removable panels for radio controls, clock, ash tray, and cigarette lighter in instrument panel. Sunshade for driver. Two coat hooks. Friction-type venti-panes, with drip shields in front doors. Lowering rear quarter windows in 2-door sedans. Lowering forward window sections in rear doors of 4-door sedans. Dual ventilators in dash panel. Package shelf below rear window. Painted step plates in door openings. Rubber floor mat and fiber board sidewall covering in luggage compartment; illumination from window in each tail light housing. Bumper jack and combination jack handle and wheel wrench.

BODY EQUIPMENT—DE LUXE MODELS

The following equipment is included in place of, or in addition to, that furnished with Special models. Except for listed variations, Convertible, Bel Air, and Station

Wagon equipment is generally identical with that of other De Luxe models:

Exterior, General: Stainless steel reveals on windshield, door windows, quarter windows, and rear window. Stainless steel moldings on front fenders and doors. Stainless steel rear fender shields. Rear fender moldings. Rear wheel cover panels.

Exterior, Convertible: Chrome plated door and quarter window frames. Folding fabric top, hydraulically operated. Lowering rear curtain (no window reveal) with slide fastener. Stainless steel drip shields.

Exterior, Bel Air: Chrome plated door and quarter window frames. Stainless steel drip molding, drip shields, and rear window divider bars.

Exterior, Station Wagon: All-steel body panels with wood-grain finish, without side or rear window reveal moldings. Body belt molding only around base of windshield and front corners. Exposed gasoline filler cap.

Interior, General: Two-tone gray color combination. Gray striped broadcloth seat upholstery, with band of plain dark gray broadcloth across top of back cushions. Foam rubber seat cushion pads. Plain light gray cloth on sidewalls. Scuff pads on rear quarter panels, as well as on all doors. Simulated carpet inserts in rubber floor mat in front compartment. Deep pile carpet in rear compartment. Two-tone gray finish on instrument panel and steering wheel. Automatic glove compartment light, ash tray, cigarette lighter, and 39-hour clock in instrument panel. Sunshades for driver and passenger. Robe cords in sedans. Arm rests, front and rear. Assist straps in 2-door sedans and sport coupe. Rear compartment ash tray in 4-door sedans, two in arm rests of other models. Stainless steel moldings on lower edge of side window garnish moldings and across tops of scuff pads. Stainless steel inserts in plastic knobs. Automatic dome light switches in front doors. Package shelf molding. Extra roof insulation. Friction-type ventipanes in rear doors of 4-door sedans. Sliding rear quarter windows in sport coupe. Etched aluminum step plates in door openings.

Interior, Convertible: Four two-tone interior color combinations to harmonize with exterior colors. Genuine deep buff leather seat upholstery and top covering on front door arm rests. Instrument panel paint and leather fabric sidewall coverings in two-tone combination of light gray and seat leather color. Garnish molding paint, front floor mat rubber and carpet inserts, and rear compartment carpet match seat leather color. Two-tone steering wheel finish of black and light gray.

Interior, Bel Air: Four two-tone interior color combinations to harmonize with exterior colors. Two-tone seat upholstery of gray, striped pile-cord fabric with genuine deep buff leather bolsters. Genuine leather top covering on front door arm rests. Gray, striped pile-cord fabric sidewall covering on lower edge of door and rear seat arm rest tops to match color of seat bolsters. Two-tone instrument panel finish in combination of light gray and leather color. Garnish moldings painted leather color with extra, bright metal moldings. Exposed bright metal roof bows. Carpet, matching leather color, on front and rear compartment floors. Two-tone steering wheel finish of black and light gray. Two rear compartment lights.

Interior, Station Wagon: Tan, simulated pig skin leather fabric seat upholstery. Wood paneling on sidewalls with brown leather fabric scuff pads. Wood grained finish on side and rear window garnish moldings. Simulated wood, leather fabric headlining and sunshade covering. Exposed roof bows with wood grained finish. Tan rubber floor mat between front and intermediate seats. Tan linoleum on floor below and behind intermediate seat. Foam rubber pad in front seat. Sliding rear quarter windows.

1951 De Luxe Fleetline 2-door Sedan

The then-advanced styling concept of the Fleetline cars had been introduced in 1942 as the two-door "Aerosedan", (the Fleetline name itself preceeded the slant-back style by one year), and remained an active and popular style. However, by 1951, both the 2-door and the 4-door models were, perhaps due to their similarity to earlier models, becoming less popular. The 4-door Fleetline Sedan was discontinued at the end of the model year, as were both Special Series models. The De Luxe Fleetline 2-door was to continue for yet another year, but by the end of 1952, the style was no longer in production.

Mr. Elmer Ryan, Bellflower, California

A new "Jet-Styled" Hood ornament appears in 1951.

The grill is restyled in keeping with Chevrolet's 1951 advertising theme of "low-lined styling".

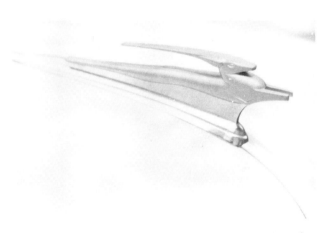

An accessory hood ornament bears a gold Impala, a feature introduced in the trim of the later 1959 Chevrolet.

The new hood emblem is restyled from 1950 (page 96).

The more rectangular shape of the upper grill bar can best be seen in this view. The earlier curved trim is seen on page 96.

This accessory bumper tip adds a pronounced flare to the appearance of the bumpers.

The Chevrolet name continues to appear on the top grill bar.

Headlamp bezels are unchanged.

A manufacturing change was made during 1950, and front fenders now display a parting line seam which runs from the headlight housing to the upper corner of the grill. This seam is absent in the 1949 and earlier 1950 fenders (page 77).

The front bumper guards are restyled for 1951.

A distinctive new semi-oval parking lamp and vent air intake duct now appears at the ends of the radiator grill.

As before, the De Luxe windshield has added bright metal trim around the windshield panes, the Special cars show only the black rubber gasket.

De Luxe cars have a long trim stripe on the sides and a matching trim at the bottom. Special series cars have only the lower trim.

The De Luxe name appears in the side trim. Special Series cars do not have a similar nameplate.

Wheels on all models are 15". Tires are blackwall 6.70 x 15, except for the Convertible on which 7.10 x 15 are furnished. Whitewall tires are an optional accessory.

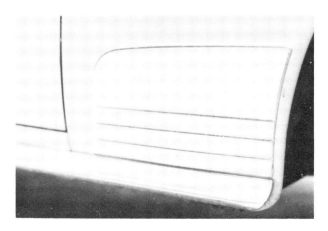

This is a chromed dress up accessory shield for the front fenders.

The belt line trim strip beneath the windows is a feature of all models, both De Luxe and Standard but the window outline trim is furnished on the De Luxe only.

The rear windows of the sedans can be lowered for ventilation, and additional vent wings in the rear doors of the 4-door sedans can be rotated open on the De Luxe Series cars only.

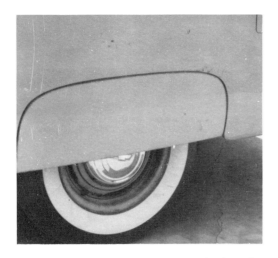

The rear wheel cover panels are standard on the De Luxe Series cars only.

The rear fenders have been restyled (see page 99), and have assumed a new shape at their rear edge. Emphasizing their new height is a new trim strip, visible above the fuel filler flap.

All models are supplied with rear fender shields. Those on the De Luxe cars are made of stainless steel; those on the Special Series are black rubber.

A new simplified trunk ornament replaces the more elaborate 1950 style. For the first time, there is no handle to grasp in lifting the lid as the concealed hinges are now spring-loaded for counterbalance.

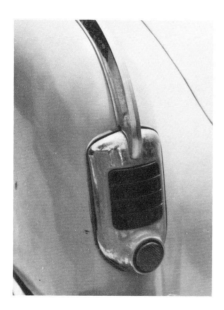

1951 tail lights assume a new shape, and above them a new trim stripe is added to emphasize the higher fender top line.

Bumper guards are restyled to add to the massive appearance.

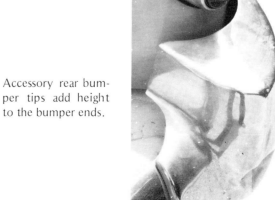

Accessory rear bumper tips add height to the bumper ends.

New this year is a license plate illuminating light built directly into the new heavier bumper at the center. This eliminates the two individual lights formerly placed on either side of the plate (page 100).

An accessory turn signal control is fastened to the steering column beneath an accessory dress-up steering wheel in this view of a 1951 De Luxe instrument panel.

The Special Series cars have the conventional three-spoke steering wheel, and the standard De Luxe series installation is a two-spoke wheel with a full-circle horn blowing ring.

A new cluster contains the instruments, but the speedometer has been removed and relocated to the right in a matching circle.

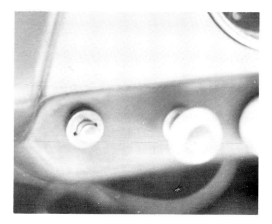

The push button for the starter is now located at the bottom of the instrument panel.

A new speedometer, in a matching case, is located to the right of the other instruments in a more pleasing panel layout.

A new round "39 hour" clock is placed at the top center of the instrument panel. The clock is standard on the De Luxe, an option on the Special Series.

The controls for the optional hot air heater are no longer suspended beneath, but protrude through the instrument panel at the left of the standard radio grill.

As previously, the ash tray is an accessory in the Special cars, but is standard in the De Luxe models.

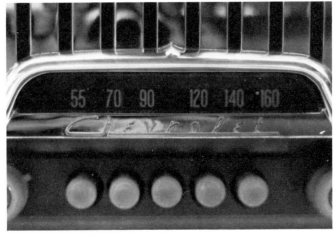

The accessory push-button radio is designed to fit into the instrument panel. When it is not furnished, a blanking panel conceals the holes for its controls.

The three-position ignition switch is flanked by Throttle and Choke control knobs.

Again the De Luxe knobs have a stainless steel insert; Special Series cars have plain plastic.

The graceful chromed inside door handle is continued.

The window crank handle knobs are plastic in the Special Series cars, and, like those on the instrument panel, plastic with a stainless steel insert on the De Luxe.

Interiors in the De Luxe closed cars are done in two-stone gray striped upholstery with a band of gray across the top of the back cushions. Special Series models are somewhat more plain, not having the contrasting upper section. Arm rests are provided in the De Luxe cars only.

America's most beautiful low-priced car

Series KK   DE LUXE
      Fleetline 2-door Sedan
      Styleline 4-door Sedan
      Styleline 2-door Sedan
      Styleline Sport Coupe
      Bel Air
      Convertible
      Station Wagon

Series KJ   SPECIAL
      Styleline 4-door Sedan
      Styleline 2-door Sedan
      Styleline Sport Coupe
      Styleline Business Coupe

Virtually unchanged for 1952, the two previous series continued. In the De Luxe, only one Fleetline model was offered, the 2-door Sedan, which would be discontinued at the end of this model year. Special Series cars were reduced to four from last year's six with the elimination of the Fleetline 2-door and 4-door.

Only a minor face-lift was done with the grill receiving a new emblem and center bar decoration, and a parking lights revision. Side trim of the De Luxe series cars was revised slightly, and the upholstery combinations of the De Luxe were reversed with dark seats capped by lighter top sections.

Although the engine ratings remained unchanged at 92 horsepower standard and a 105 hp version for use with the Powerglide automatic transmission, their mounts were relocated from the front to a point about 12" back for better balance in the chassis.

SPECIFICATIONS

POWER PLANT

Engine Type: 6-cylinder, valve-in-head 216.5 cu. in. displacement. Bore x stroke, 3½ x 3¾ in. Compression ratio, 6.6:1. Horsepower, 92 at 3400 rpm.
Pistons: Lightweight cast alloy iron, with slipper skirt. Surfaces treated to resist wear. Three rings, all above pin.
Crankshaft: Drop-forged steel. Counterbalanced. Rubber-floated harmonic balancer.
Main Bearings: Four, thin-wall babbitt, precision interchangeable.
Lubrication System: Four-way: (1) pressure streams to connecting rod bearings, (2) full pressure to main and camshaft bearings and timing gears, (3) metered pressure to valve mechanism, (4) splash to cylinder walls. Gear pump. Crankcase ventilator. Refill capacity, 5 qts.
Fuel System: Single throat, down-draft carburetor; concentric float bowl, vacuum fuel enrichment valve, enclosed accelerator pump with fuel-lubricated piston, manual choke, with fast-idle mechanism. Air cleaner. Thermostatic manifold heat control. Octane Selector. 16-gallon tank. Overflow alarm. and concealed filler in sedans and coupes.
Cooling System: Pressure type with four-pound cap. Ribbed cellular radiator. Self-adjusting seal, and permanently lubricated water pump. Thermostatic heat control. Nozzle-jet valve seat cooling. Water jackets full-length of piston stroke around all cylinders. Capacity, 15 qts.
Electrical System: Automatic spark control. Sealed ignition coil. 14 mm spark plugs. High-output ventilated generator, with current and voltage regulators. Solenoid-operated push-button starter, with positive shift.
Clutch: Ventilated, diaphragm spring type, with permanently lubricated ball throwout bearing.
Transmission: Three-speed Synchro-Mesh. Steering column gearshift. Gear ratios: Low and reverse, 2.94:1; intermediate, 1.68:1; high, 1:1.
Power Plant Mounting. Rubber-cushioned, 3-point. High side mountings.

CHASSIS

Frame: Full-length box-girder type. Extra reinforcements in Bel Air. Special VK structure of I-beams in frame of Convertible.
Front Suspension: Unitized Knee Action. Life-sealed double-acting shock absorbers. Ride stabilizer.
Rear Suspension: Rubber-cushioned semi-elliptic springs. Metal covers with fabric. Tension-type shackle mountings. Life-sealed, double-acting shock absorbers, mounted diagonally.
Rear Axle: Hypoid, semi-floating, with six ball and roller bearings. Ratio, 4.11:1.
Drive System: Torque tube, with fully enclosed universal joint and tubular propeller shaft.
Brakes: Hydraulic, self-energizing. Bonded linings. 11-inch drums, with cast alloy iron braking surfaces. Mechanical actuation of rear brakes for parking.
Steering: Centerpoint. Semi-reversible type gear, ratio, 19.4:1.
Wheels: Short-spoke, steel disk. Wide base rims.
Tires: Extra-low pressure type. 6.70-15-4 ply. (Station Wagon—6.70-15-6 ply.)
Exterior Dimensions (nominal): Wheelbase, 115 inches. Over-all length, 197⅞ inches. Over-all width, 74 inches.

Chassis Equipment: Bumper and guards. Front license guard. Front fender moldings on De Luxe Series. Gravel deflectors, front and rear. Bumper jack. Jack handle and wheel wrench.

LIGHTS—HORN—BATTERY

Lights: Thermal circuit-breaker-protected lighting system. Sealed beam headlights; beam indicator on speedometer. Parking lights in radiator grille. Tail and stop lights with separate reflector buttons. Rear license light. Single tail, stop, and license light on Station Wagon, automatically positioned with tail gate. Dome light, with manual switch; except Bel Air which has sidelights — automatic switch at each front door in De Luxe Series. Matched horns.
Battery: Fifteen-plate, 100 ampere-hour.

INSTRUMENT PANEL—CONTROLS—VISION

Instruments: Speedometer, oil pressure and gasoline gauges, battery charge and engine heat indicators. Adjustable indirect lighting.
Controls: Two-spoke steering wheel, with full-circle horn-blowing ring, De Luxe Series; three-spoke wheel, with horn button, Special Series. Rubber-padded clutch, brake, and accelerator pedals; foot-controlled headlight dimmer switch. Illuminated three-position ignition lock switch. Ivory plastic control knobs, with bright metal inserts in De Luxe Series. Finger-tip gearshift lever. L-handle for parking brake.
Vision: Two windshield wipers. Two full-width windshield defroster openings. Two adjustable sunshades in De Luxe Series; one in Special Series. Adjustable rear view mirror.

BODIES

General Features: Fisher Unisteel construction with integral rear fenders, welded-in instrument panel, and solid steel underbody. Turret top, except hydraulically operated folding top on Convertible. Thorough insulation. Polished pyroxylin lacquer finish. Safety plate glass, except vinyl plastic rear window in Convertible. Large, sloping, curved windshield. Friction-type ventipanes for No Draft ventilation, with drip shields in front doors of all Turret Top models. Lowering windows in all doors. Lowering rear quarter windows in two-door sedans, Bel Air, and Convertible; sliding in De Luxe Sport Coupe and Station Wagon. Friction-type ventipanes in rear doors of De Luxe four-door sedan. Dual ventilators in dash panel, individually controlled. Inclined plane front seat adjustment. Push-button door handles, with key locks in both front doors. Concealed door hinges.
Exterior Decoration and Equipment: Bright metal moldings on body sill, belt line, and windshield divider. Bright metal ventipane frames. In addition in De Luxe Series: bright metal moldings on doors, rear fenders, windshield reveal, side window reveals of sedans and Sport Coupe, rear window reveal of sedans, Sport Coupe, and Bel Air; and rear window dividers of Bel Air; bright metal rear fender shields (black rubber in Special Series); rear wheel cover panels.
Interior Appointments: Chrome-plated, low-hub hardware. Rear seat foot rest in floor panel. Two coat hooks in sedans, sport coupes, and business coupe. Package shelf in sedans, coupes, and Bel Air, with metal molding in De Luxe sedans and Sport Coupe. Etched aluminum step plates in De Luxe Series; painted steel in Special Series. Leather fabric scuff pads on doors and rear quarter panels.

In addition, in De Luxe Series: foam rubber cushion pads in front seats and in rear seats of sedans and coupes; front arm rests in all models; rear arm rests in sedans and coupes; rear compartment ash tray in four-door sedan and Station Wagon, one in each arm rest of two-door sedans and coupes; bright metal moldings across tops of scuff pads; and across lower edge of side window garnish moldings in sedans and coupes; extra sound insulation on roof panel of sedans, Sport Coupe, and Bel Air; bright metal side window frames in Bel Air and Convertible; and exposed roof bows with bright metal finish in Bel Air and with wood finish in Station Wagon.
Luggage Compartment Features of sedans and coupes: Counterbalanced, automatically locking deck lid, with concealed hinges. Black leather-grained sidewall trim and rubber floor mat. Illuminated from window in each tail light housing. Spare wheel and tire mounted vertically in well at right side. Hold-down spring to retain tools. Station Wagon has 4 doors—center and rear seats removable for extra luggage space.

COLORS—UPHOLSTERY

Exterior Colors: Nine colors and four two-tone combinations for sedans, sport coupes, and business coupe; four colors and eleven two-tone combinations for Bel Air; ten paint colors and five top fabric colors for Convertible; and four colors in combination with wood grain finish for Station Wagon.
Upholstery: De Luxe Series interiors color-correlated with exteriors; seat upholstery of chevron pattern cloth with plain broadcloth in sedans and Sport Coupe, of novelty pattern cloth with genuine deep-buff leather in Bel Air and of full genuine deep-buff leather in Convertible and of leather fabric with pig-skin finish in Station Wagon. Two-tone gray interiors in Special Series, with seat upholstery of checked pattern cloth.

Special features of De Luxe models with automatic drive.

Engine Type: 235.5 cubic inch displacement. Bore x stroke, 3⁹⁄₁₆ x 3¹¹⁄₁₆ inches. Compression ratio, 6.7:1. Horsepower, 105 at 3600 rpm.
Piston Rings: One twist-type and one taper-face compression ring, one wide-slot oil control ring.
Valve Mechanism: Self-adjusting hydraulic valve lifters.
Fuel System: Automatic choke.
Cooling System: Transmission oil cooler.
Transmission: Automatic, hydraulic torque converter, with planetary gears for reverse and emergency low. Manual selector for hydraulic control of transmission; mechanical parking lock control. Safety switch in starter circuit. Maximum torque converter ratio, 2.2:1. Planetary gear ratio, 1.82:1. Over-all ratios: Drive, 2.2:1; Low and Reverse, 4:1. Refill capacity, 9 qts.
Rear Axle: Ratio, 3.55:1.
Tires: 7.10-15—4-ply on Convertible.

1952 De Luxe Convertible

Production of the familar-looking Fleetline 2-door Sedan was ended in 1952. Introduced in 1942 as the Aerosedan, the style was immediately popular, but as the years wore on, its appearance became obsolescent and the model was finally retired this year.

1952 De Luxe Fleetline 2-door Sedan

Mr. Jeff Mansfield, San Diego, California

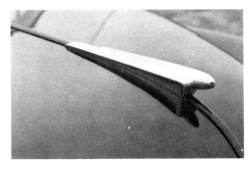

The sweeping "wings" of last year's hood ornament are gone and a new configuration appears.

Only the grill trim and emblems are changed to mark the 1952 model.

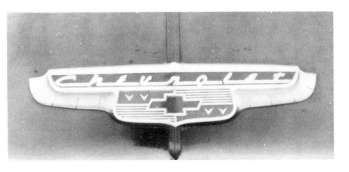

The new hood emblem now has more gently rounded wings and the name is prominently displayed.

Accessory bumper tips add extra "flare" to change the appearance of the stock bumper.

Five vertical trim caps are added to the center bar of the grill and add interest in that area.

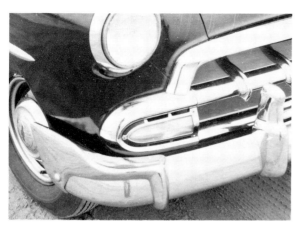

Greatly resembling this same view of the 1951 model, a different parking light assembly (below) and the added vertical trim on the center grill bar are points of difference.

The visible seam in the fender running from the headlight to the corner of the grill remains in evidence.

Replacing the 1951 parking light and its associated trim (page 113) is a new wider lens.

The sporty appearance of a Convertible is emphasized with a lowered top and elevated sun visors.

Blackwall tires continue as standard in size 6:70 x 15. All tires are 4 ply except for those on the Station Wagon which are six ply. The beauty rings on the wheels are accessories, but the hub caps are correct for all models.

A De Luxe nameplate is positioned on the rear fender above a standard stainless steel decorative trim plate. Both items, and the trim stripe trailing down the fender are used on the De Luxe cars only. Special Series car have a smaller but similar fender guard in black rubber.

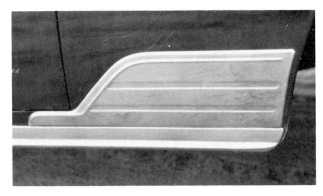

This stainless steel decorative trim is a dress-up accessory trim added to match the standard item on the rear fenders.

The bright metal mouldings at the belt line, the body sill, and the windshield divider are standard on all cars. The body and fender stripes are a feature of the De Luxe series only.

Rear wheel cover panels (fender "skirts") are standard on all models in the De Luxe Series and have been removed from this car. Special Series cars do not have the panels.

The unchanged outside door handle is given a new look with the addition of an accessory dress-up trim.

Tail lights are unchanged, but the omission of the trim strip used above them in 1951 (page 117) gives a new look. The use of a separate reflector button at the bottom of the light is continued.

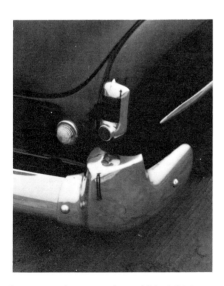

Accessory bumper tips add height to the bumper ends.

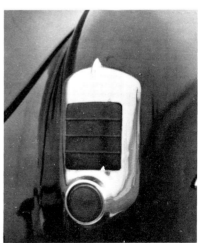

1952

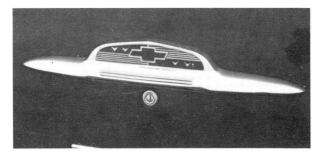

A new trunk lid ornament now places the bow tie insignia in a novel field above winged extensions.

The accessory bumper guard does not limit access to the luggage compartment.

The small rear window, formerly used in the Convertible, became a one-piece transparent zippered flap in 1951.

As is evident in this view, the top line of the rear fenders has been raised substantially (compare page 99), in keeping with a continuing styling trend towards "tailfins".

The back up lamps are an accessory. These same lamps are later used as parking lights on the initial Corvette.

An accessory dress-up trim is added to emphasize the appearance of the gas tank flap on the left rear fender.

The lowered top of the Convertible disappears almost entirely below the body line. Ringing the top storage compartment are fasteners to which a canvas cover is snapped to conceal the folded top.

A standard mirror, mounted to the windshield divider, has been replaced with this no-glare two-position accessory.

The genuine leather upholstery of the Convertible is suited to the open-air configuration.

The two-spoke steering wheel with its full circle horn blowing ring is continued in the De Luxe models. A restyled medallion at the hub bears a distinctive pattern.

A graceful trim stripe curves across the door panel of the Convertible.

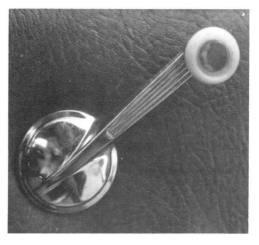

Behind the handles may be seen the leather-like upholstery material used on the door panels of the Convertible.

All De Luxe series cars are furnished with two sun visors, the Special Series cars have only one for the driver.

Convertibles are upholstered in genuine leather, the only models to be so upholstered. Station Wagons have a pig-skin finish artificial leather; the sedans and coupes are done in broadcloth or other conventional materials.

1952

An L-shaped handle is continued on the parking brake which is located to the right of the steering column.

The Instrument cluster provides needed information and is located just to the left in front of the driver. To the right, connected by a serrated trim strip in the De Luxe models, is the speedometer, also a large, clearly visible instrument. The strip between the instruments is not used in Special Series cars.

A five push button radio continues unchanged.

The ash tray has become standard in both Series.

Heater and defroster controls, when the accessory is ordered, protrude through slots at the left side of the instrument panel.

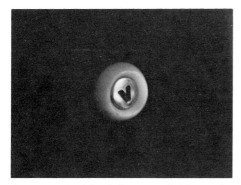

A vent control knob is suspended beneath the instrument panel at the right side of the instrument panel matching another on the left.

A new three-position ignition lock permits operation of the car without an ignition key. To lock the ignition, it is necessary that the key be withdrawn in the LOCK position. To its left is the windshield wiper knob, below it can be seen the control knob for the Convertible's automatic top.

1953 CHEVROLET

Entirely NEW through and through!

Series C   THE BEL AIR SERIES
    4-door Sedan
    2-door Sedan
    Sport Coupe
    Convertible

Series B   THE TWO-TEN Series
    4-door Sedan
    2-door Sedan
    Club Coupe
    Sport Coupe
    Handyman (6-passenger station wagon)
    Townsman (8-passenger station wagon; wood-
       grain trim)

Series A   THE ONE-FIFTY SERIES
    4-door Sedan
    2-door Sedan
    Club Coupe
    Business Coupe
    Handyman (economy 6-passenger station wagon)

With its second all-new post war design, Chevrolet brought three model-line selections to the 1953 market. At the top was the new Bel Air Series, most luxurious of the three, which was now expanded to include two sedans and a Convertible in addition to the earlier trend-setting style now called a "Sport Coupe". The mid-range line, the Two-Ten Series, was slightly scaled down in appointments, although it too had exterior bright metal trim, and standard arm rests, horn ring, cigarette lighter, ash tray, and dual sun visors. At the bottom was the "economy" model, the One-Fifty, which included a minimum of trim but shared the same body shell and chassis with the others.

A new wrap-around windshield replaced the earlier split windshield, and all but the One-Fifty series and the Two-Ten Club Coupe also had a wide wrap around rear window similar to that introduced earlier on the Bel Air.

An exciting new option, Power Steering, was offered for the first time.

The standard engine was now rated at 108 horsepower at 3600 rpm, and had a bore and stroke of 3-9/16 x 3-15/16. This 235.5 cubic inch engine continued to use the cast iron pistons for which Chevrolet was famed, and had a compression ratio of 7.1:1, a bit higher than the Powerglide engine of 1952. For cars incorporating Powerglide, an even higher 7.5:1 compression ratio was used, and with other modifications, including aluminum pistons, this engine was rated at 115 horsepower at 3600 rpm.

In January of 1953 at their Motorama promotional automobile show, General Motors showed "dream cars" from several of the Divisions, including Chevrolet. The Corvette, as Chevrolet's entry was called, was acclaimed at once by the public, so much so that plans were made to place it into immediate production. By July the first "production" model was completed, but through the second half of calendar 1953, only approximately 300 were completed at Flint. True production commenced on January 1st, 1954 in St. Louis where Corvette production has remained ever since. For an in-depth study of the Chevrolet Sports Car, readers are directed to the author's *The Real CORVETTE*, #3 of The Chevy Chase Series.

S P E C I F I C A T I O N S

Note that detail specifications of models equipped with "Blue-Flame 125" valve-in-head engine and Powerglide Automatic Transmission are described in box below.

POWER PLANT

Engine Type: 6-cylinder, valve-in-head 235.5 cu. in. displacement. Bore x stroke, 3⁹⁄₁₆ x 3¹⁵⁄₁₆ in. Compression ratio, 7.5:1. Horsepower, 115 at 3700 rpm.

Pistons: Aluminum Alloy, controlled thermo expansion, offset pin. Surfaces treated with a wear resistant coating. Three rings, all above pin.

Crankshaft: Drop-forged steel. Counterbalanced. Rubber-floated harmonic balancer.

Main Bearings: Four, thin-wall babbitt, precision interchangeable.

Lubrication System: Full pressure to main, connecting rod, camshaft bearings, and timing gears; metered pressure to valve mechanism, also oil is metered to cylinder walls and piston pins by a hole in connecting rod bearing boss.

Fuel System: Single throat, down-draft carburetor. Concentric float bowl, vacuum fuel enrichment valve, enclosed accelerator pump with fuel-lubricated piston, automatic choke with fast-idle mechanism. Air cleaner. Thermostatic manifold heat control. Octane Selector. 16-gallon tank. Concealed filler in sedans and coupes.

Cooling System: By-pass type, with seven-pound pressure cap. Ribbed cellular radiator. Self-adjusting seal, and permanently lubricated water pump. Thermostatic heat control. Water jackets full-length around all cylinders. Capacity, 16 qts.

Electrical System: Automatic spark control. Sealed ignition coil. 14 mm spark plugs. High-output ventilated generator, with current and voltage regulator. 45-ampere generator.

Clutch: Ventilated, diaphragm spring type, with permanently lubricated ball throwout bearing.

Transmission: Three-speed Synchro-Mesh. Steering column gearshift. Gear ratios: Low and reverse, 2.94:1; intermediate, 1.68:1; high, 1:1.

Power Plant Mounting: Rubber-cushioned, 3-point. High side mountings.

CHASSIS

Frame: Full-length box-girder type. Extra reinforcements Sport Coupe. Special VK structure of I-beams in frame of Convertible.

Front Suspension: Unitized Knee Action. Life-sealed double-acting shock absorbers. Ride stabilizer.

Rear Suspension: Rubber-cushioned semi-elliptic springs. Tension-type shackle mountings. Life-sealed, double-acting shock absorbers, mounted diagonally.

Rear Axle: Hypoid, semi-floating, with six ball and roller bearings. Ratio, 3.7:1.

Drive System: Torque tube, with fully enclosed universal joint and tubular propeller shaft.

Brakes: Hydraulic, self-energizing. Bonded linings. 11-inch drums, with cast alloy iron braking surfaces. Mechanical actuation of rear brakes for parking.

Steering: Centerpoint. Semi-reversible type gear; ratio, 19.4:1.

Wheels: Short-spoke, steel disk. 5" rims.

Tires: Extra-low pressure type. 6.70-15-4 ply rating. (Townsman—6.70-15-6 ply rating.)

Exterior Dimensions (nominal): Wheelbase, 115 inches. Over-all length, 195 inches; station wagons 198¼ inches. Over-all width, 74¾ inches.

Chassis Equipment: Bumpers and guards. Rear license guard. Front fender moldings on Bel Air and "Two-Ten" Series. Gravel deflectors, front and rear. Bumper jack, jack handle and wheel wrench.

LIGHTS—HORN—BATTERY

Lights: Thermal circuit-breaker-protected lighting system. Sealed beam headlights, beam indicator on speedometer. Parking lights in radiator grille. Tail and stop lights with reflex type lens. Rear license light. Dome light, with manual switch; except Sport Coupe which has two sidelights. Automatic interior lighting switch at each front door in Bel Air and "Two-Ten" Series. Matched horns.

Battery: Fifteen-plate, 100 ampere-hour.

INSTRUMENT PANEL—CONTROLS—VISION

Instruments: Speedometer, oil pressure and gasoline gauges, battery charge and engine heat indicators. Adjustable indirect lighting.

Controls: Two-spoke steering wheel, with full-circle horn-ring in Bel Air and "Two-Ten" Series; horn button in "One-Fifty" Series. Rubber-padded clutch, brake and accelerator pedals; foot-controlled headlight dimmer switch. Three-position key-starter ignition lock switch. Plastic control knobs, with bright metal inserts in Bel Air and "Two-Ten" Series. Finger-tip gearshift lever. T-handle for parking brake.

Vision: Two windshield wipers. Full-width windshield defroster openings. Two adjustable sunshades in Bel Air and "Two-Ten" Series; one in "One-Fifty" Series. Adjustable inside rear view mirror.

BODIES

General Features: Fisher Unisteel construction with integral rear fenders, welded-in instrument panel, and solid steel underbody. Turret top, except hydraulically operated folding top on Convertible. Thorough insulation. Polished lacquer finish. Safety plate glass, except vinyl plastic rear window in Convertible and safety sheet side door windows in "One-Fifty" Station Wagon. Large, one-piece curved windshield. Crank-operated ventipanes with drip shields on front doors of all models. Lowering windows in all doors. Lowering rear quarter windows in two door sedans, Sport Coupe, Club Coupe and Convertible; sliding in Townsman Station Wagon. Dual ventilators in dash panel, individually controlled. Inclined plane front seat adjustment. Push-button door handles, with key locks in both front doors. Concealed door hinges.

Exterior Decoration and Equipment: Bright metal moldings on belt line. Bright metal ventipane frames. In addition in Bel Air and "Two-Ten" Series: bright metal moldings on body sill, doors, front fenders, windshield reveal, side window reveals of sedans and Club Coupe, rear window reveal of sedans, Club Coupe, and Sport Coupe; bright metal rear fender shields (black rubber in "One-Fifty" Series). Additional on Bel Air Series only: Bright metal double moldings with series name and crest on rear fender, extra-wide window reveals on sedans, windshield pillar cover and saddle moldings on Sport Coupe and Convertible. Rear wheel cover panel.

Interior Appointments: Chrome-plated, low-hub hardware. Rear seat foot rest in floor panel. Two coat hooks in sedans, Club Coupe, and utility sedans. Rolled embossed step plates. Leather fabric scuff pads on doors and rear quarter panels, bright metal in "Two-Ten" Club Coupe, Bel Air and "Two-Ten" Station Wagons. In addition, in Bel Air and "Two-Ten" Series: foam rubber cushion pads in front seats and in rear seats of sedans and coupes; front arm rests in all models; rear arm rests in sedans and coupes; rear compartment ash tray in four-door sedans; one in each arm rest of two-door sedans and coupes; bright metal moldings on doors and rear quarter panels. Extra sound insulation on roof panel of sedans, Club Coupe and Sport Coupe; bright metal side window frames in Sport Coupe and Convertible, and exposed roof bows with bright metal finish in Bel Air Sport Coupe.

Luggage Compartment features of sedans and coupes: Counterbalanced, automatically locking deck lid, with concealed hinges. Sidewall trim and rubber floor mat. Spare wheel and tire mounted vertically in well at right side. Hold-down spring to retain tools. All Station Wagons have four doors. Extra carrying space provided in 8-passenger Townsman by removable center and rear seats—in 6-passenger Handyman ("One-Fifty" and "Two-Ten" models) by folding rear seat.

Special Features of Models with Powerglide

Engine: Horsepower 125 at 4000 r.p.m. Self-adjusting hydraulic valve lifters.

Cooling System: Includes transmission oil cooler.

Transmission: Automatic, hydraulic, three-element torque converter, with planetary gears for reverse and automatic low. Manual selector for hydraulic control of transmission. Safety switch in starter circuit. Maximum torque converter ratio, 2.1 to 1. Planetary gear ratio, 1.82 to 1. Over-all Ratio, 3.82 to 1.

Tires: 7.10-15-4 ply rating on Convertibles.

Rear Axle: Ratio, 3.55 to 1.

1953 One-Fifty Handyman   *Mr. Philip Donner, Carlsbad, California*

Rear wheel cover panels are missing.

1953 Bel Air Sport Coupe

1953 Two-Ten Club Coupe

Mr. Robert Nightingale, Jr.
San Diego, California

Mrs. Ruth Schmeiser   *Oceanside, California*

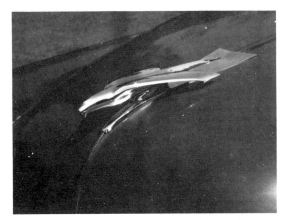

A new hood ornament appears and is used on all three Series.

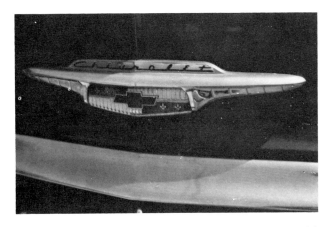

The hood emblem again changes, growing graceful "wings".

The center grill bar now has three, rather than the previous five, vertical fins, and the rounded ends of the upper grill bar soften its former angularity.

New bumper guards appear, having a more massive appearance than the earlier style.

Grill ends are decoratively embossed.

A new headlight door with a fold to blend with the fender line appears in 1953.

A crease now runs the length of the car from the headlight past the mid-section. In addition, the Bel Air and the Two-Ten Series cars have a bright metal side moulding which is omitted on the One-Ten Series. Tire size on all models is 6.70 x 15.

Familiar round parking lights again appears in 1953, their size exaggerated by a surrounding bezel.

The one-piece curved windshield now appears on all models. The ONE-FIFTY Series has a black rubber gasket showing surrounding, the TWO-TEN and BEL AIR have a bright trim over that (right and above right), and the BEL AIR SPORT COUPE (only) has an added windshield pillar bright metal trim (left and left above).

Contra-rotating windshield wipers lie flat on the cowl.

New sliding vent locks are used this year replacing the rotating latch of 1952 bodies (page 132).

When the optional radio is installed, its four-section antenna is located on the left front fender.

The outside mirror is an accessory.

The inside rear view mirror is standard, and is suspended from above the windshield moulding (left) except in the Bel Air Sport Coupe where it is attached to the instrument panel (above).

Two-Ten 4-door Sedan

Two-Ten Club Coupe

Bel Air Sport Coupe

On the Bel Air Series only, a dual stripe appears on the rear fenders encompassing the series name. The bright metal fender guards are used also on the Two-Ten Series, but those on the One-Fifty are black rubber. Rear fender panels are standard on the Bel Air and are absent in this photo.

The rear quarter roof pillar slants slightly forward in Bel Air and Two-Ten Sport Coupes giving a somewhat rakish appearance to this area.

Push-button outside door handles with integral locks are used on both front doors of all models.

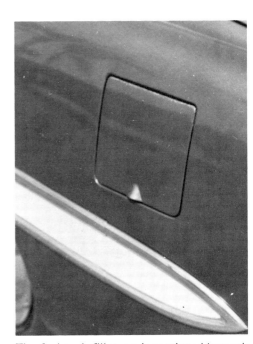

The fuel tank filler cap is continued beneath the left rear fender under a hinged flap.

Only the Two-Ten Club Coupe (and all One-Fifty sedans and coupes) still use this earlier-style rear window.

When applicable, the POWERGLIDE name is impressed into the new rear deck lid emblem. A similar emblem, without the word, is used on cars not incorporating the accessory.

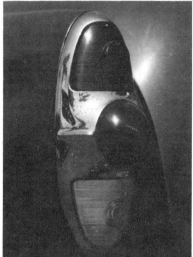

New for 1953 is a tail light into which optional back-up lights can be incorporated.

The new bumper guards are standard on all models as is the rear license plate guard which appears on all models except the station wagons.

Bel Air Sport Coupe

Two-Ten Club Coupe. Steering wheel leather glove is an accessory.

A new instrument panel layout appears in 1953.

Both the Bel Air and the Two-Ten series are furnished with two-spoke steering wheels with full-circle horn blowing ring. The One-Fifty models do not have the horn ring, merely a horn button at the hub.

A black plastic knob is used on the shift lever.

When optional Powerglide is installed, a position indicator appears on the column just below the steering wheel.

A large new speedometer is now placed directly in the driver's line of vision. Top speed is calibrated to 110 miles per hour against 100 mph earlier.

The oil pressure, gasoline gauge, battery charge, and engine heat indicators are standard in all models. During 1953 a change in the oil pressure was made necessitating a similar change in the gauge. Note 0-30 psi full scale above, 0-60 psi left. Directional signals, still optional, incorporate the arrow-indicators shown on the panels.

The electric clock is standard in the Bel Air series, an option in the others.

A script nameplate appears at the top center of the instrument panel.

A locking package compartment is provided in all models.

One of two optional accessory radios, the Push Button Custom Deluxe Radio is available at higher price.

A lower-priced Custom Radio is also optionally available but lacks the push-button tuning feature.

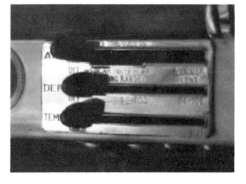

Returning to a position at the bottom of the instrument panel, the built-in controls for the optional heater are placed to the right of the ignition switch. This is the control for the Air Flow Heater and Defroster unit which utilizes outside air for full ventilation. An alternate option, the Recirculating Heater/Defroster merely heats and circulates the air already in the car.

Unlike the rear quarter windows of the other models (including the Sport Coupes) which may be cranked open for ventilation, those in the other Coupes can not. On the Two-Ten Club Coupe, shown here, this window slides and is fitted with an operating grip. The Coupes of the One-Fifty Series have fixed rear quarter windows.

The use of bright metal inserts in the plastic knobs of the window cranks is continued in the Bel Air and Two-Ten series only. The One-Ten Series cars have plain plastic knobs.

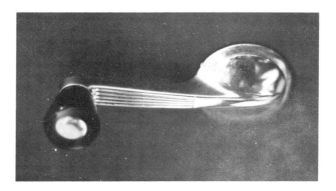

The BEL AIR SERIES
   4-door Sedan
   2-door Sedan
   Sport Coupe
   Convertible
   Townsman (8-passenger station wagon)

The TWO-TEN SERIES
   4-door Sedan
   2-door Sedan
   Club Coupe
   Handyman (6-passenger station wagon)

The ONE-FIFTY SERIES
   4-door Sedan
   2-door Sedan
   Utility Sedan (formerly the Business Coupe)
   Handyman (economy 6-passenger station wagon)

Continuing on the 115 inch wheelbase chassis introduced in 1949, the 1954 Chevrolets were largely face-lifted versions of the 1953 models. The three Series of the previous year were continued, but with some modifications. The BEL AIR SERIES gained a luxury station wagon, the Townsman, which was up-graded from the TWO-TEN SERIES. The Convertible and the Sport Coupe were eliminated from the TWO-TEN SERIES, and the ONE-FIFTY SERIES lost its Club Coupe and its Business Coupe became a "Utility Sedan" with more storage space behind the single front seat.

In addition to the optional Power Steering, first offered in 1953, Power-operated windows and front seats became available as options, and the big news, although quietly noted, was the substitution of aluminum pistons in the standard engine, marking the death of the original "cast iron wonder".

Again two engines were available. The "Blue Flame 125", used with the optional Powerglide transmission featured high-lift cam and hydraulic lifters and a 125 horsepower rating. Powerglide itself was available for the first time on all models, the One-Fifty series as well as the Two-Ten and the Bel Air. The standard engine, called the "Blue Flame 115" now had aluminum pistons, featured full-pressure lubrication, and like the Blue Flame 125, had a 7.5:1 compression ratio.

As previously noted, on January 1st, 1954, the Chevrolet St. Louis Assembly Plant commenced the production of Chevrolet's new sports car, the Corvette. More complete information regarding this fibre-glass bodied unique Chevrolet model will be found in the author's *The Real CORVETTE*, which is Volume 3 of this series.

S P E C I F I C A T I O N S

Note that detail specifications of "Two-Ten" and Bel Air models equipped with new 115 h.p. "Blue-Flame" valve-in-head engine and Powerglide Automatic Transmission are described in box below.

POWER PLANT

Engine Type: 6-cylinder, valve-in-head 235.5 cu. in. displacement. Bore x stroke, 3⁹/₁₆ x 3¹⁵/₁₆ in. Compression ratio, 7.1:1. Horsepower, 108 at 3600 rpm.

Pistons: Lightweight cast alloy iron, with slipper skirt. Surfaces treated to resist wear. Three rings, all above pin.

Crankshaft: Drop-forged steel. Counterbalanced. Rubber-floated harmonic balancer.

Main Bearings: Four, thin-wall babbitt, precision interchangeable.

Lubrication System: Four-way: (1) pressure streams to connecting rod bearings, (2) full pressure to main and camshaft bearings and timing gears, (3) metered pressure to valve mechanism, (4) splash to cylinder walls. Gear pump. Crankcase ventilator. Refill capacity, 5 qts.

Fuel System: Single throat, down-draft carburetor; concentric float bowl, vacuum fuel enrichment valve, enclosed accelerator pump with fuel-lubricated piston, automatic choke with fast-idle mechanism. Air cleaner. Thermostatic manifold heat control. Octane Selector. 16-gallon tank. Concealed filler in sedans and coupes.

Cooling System: By-pass type, with four-pound pressure cap. Ribbed cellular radiator. Self-adjusting seal, and permanently lubricated water pump. Thermostatic heat control. Water jackets full-length around all cylinders. Capacity, 15 qts.

Electrical System: Automatic spark control. Sealed ignition coil. 14 mm spark plugs. High-output ventilated generator, with current and voltage regulators. 45 ampere generator.

Clutch: Ventilated, diaphragm spring type, with permanently lubricated ball throwout bearing.

Transmission: Three-speed Synchro-Mesh. Steering column gearshift. Gear ratios: Low and reverse, 2.94:1; intermediate, 1.68:1; high, 1:1.

Power Plant Mounting: Rubber-cushioned, 3-point. High side mountings.

CHASSIS

Frame: Full-length box-girder type. Extra reinforcements in Sport Coupe. Special VK structure of I-beams in frame of Convertible.

Front Suspension: Unitized Knee Action. Life-sealed double-acting shock absorbers. Ride stabilizer.

Rear Suspension: Rubber-cushioned semi-elliptic springs. Tension-type shackle mountings. Life-sealed double-acting shock absorbers, mounted diagonally.

Rear Axle: Hypoid, semi-floating, with six ball and roller bearings. Ratio, 3.7:1.

Drive System: Torque tube, with fully enclosed universal joint and tubular propeller shaft.

Brakes: Hydraulic, self-energizing. Bonded linings. 11-inch drums, with cast alloy iron braking surfaces. Mechanical actuation of rear brakes for parking.

Steering: Centerpoint. Semi-reversible type gear; ratio, 19.4:1.

Wheels: Short-spoke, steel disk. 5" rims.

Tires: Extra-low pressure type. 6.70-15-4 ply rating. (Townsman—6.70-15-6 ply rating.)

Exterior Dimensions (nominal): Wheelbase, 115 inches. Over-all length, 195½ inches. Over-all width, 74¾ inches.

Chassis Equipment: Bumpers and guards. Rear license guard. Front fender moldings on Bel Air and "Two-Ten" Series. Gravel deflectors, front and rear. Bumper jack, jack handle and wheel wrench.

LIGHTS—HORN—BATTERY

Lights: Thermal circuit-breaker-protected lighting system. Sealed beam headlights, beam indicator on speedometer. Parking lights in radiator grille. Tail and stop lights with reflex type lens. Rear license light. Dome light, with manual switch; except Sport Coupe which has two sidelights. Automatic interior lighting switch at each front door in Bel Air and "Two-Ten" Series. Matched horns.

Battery: Fifteen-plate, 100 ampere-hour.

INSTRUMENT PANEL—CONTROLS—VISION

Instruments: Speedometer, oil pressure and gasoline gauges, battery charge and engine heat indicators. Adjustable indirect lighting.

Controls: Two-spoke steering wheel, with full-circle horn-ring in Bel Air and "Two-Ten" Series; horn button in "One-Fifty" Series. Rubber-padded clutch, brake and accelerator pedals; foot-controlled headlight dimmer switch. Three-position key-starter ignition lock switch. Plastic control knobs, with bright metal inserts in Bel Air and "Two-Ten" Series. Finger-tip gearshift lever. T-handle for parking brake.

Vision: Two windshield wipers. Two full-width windshield defroster openings. Two adjustable sunshades in Bel Air and "Two-Ten" Series; one in "One-Fifty" Series. Adjustable inside rear view mirror.

BODIES

General Features: Fisher Unisteel construction with integral rear fenders, welded-in instrument panel, and solid steel underbody. Turret top, except hydraulically operated folding top on Convertible. Thorough insulation. Polished lacquer finish. Safety plate glass, except vinyl plastic rear window in Convertible and safety sheet side door windows in "One-Fifty" Station Wagon. Large, one-piece curved windshield. Crank-operated ventipanes with drip shields on front doors of all models. Lowering windows in all doors. Lowering rear quarter windows in two-door sedans, Sport Coupes and Convertibles; sliding in Townsman Station Wagon and "Two-Ten" Club Coupe. Friction-type ventipanes in rear doors of Bel Air and "Two-Ten" four-door sedans. Dual ventilators in dash panel, individually controlled. Inclined plane front seat adjustment. Push-button door handles, with key locks in both front doors. Concealed door hinges.

Exterior Decoration and Equipment: Bright metal moldings on belt line. Bright metal ventipane frames. In addition in Bel Air and "Two-Ten" Series: bright metal moldings on body sill, doors, rear fenders, windshield reveal, side window reveals of sedans and Club Coupe, rear window reveal of sedans, Club Coupe, and Sport Coupes; bright metal rear fender shields (black rubber in "One-Fifty" Series). Additional on Bel Air Series only: Bright metal double moldings with series name and crest on rear fender, extra-wide window reveals on sedans, windshield pillar cover and saddle moldings on Sport Coupe and Convertible. Rear wheel cover panels.

Interior Appointments: Chrome-plated, low-hub hardware. Rear seat foot rest in all models. Two coat hooks in sedans, Club Coupes, and business coupe. Rolled embossed step plates. Leather fabric scuff pads on doors and rear quarter panels, bright metal in "Two-Ten" Station Wagons. In addition, in Bel Air and "Two-Ten" Series: foam rubber cushion pads in front seats and in rear seats of sedans and coupes; front arm rests in all models; rear arm rests in sedans and coupes; rear compartment ash tray in four-door sedans; one in each arm rest of two-door sedans and coupes; bright metal moldings on doors and rear quarter panels. Extra sound insulation on roof panel of sedans, Club Coupe, and Sport Coupes; bright metal side window frames in Sport Coupes and Convertibles; exposed roof bows with bright metal finish in Bel Air Sport Coupe.

Luggage Compartment features of sedans and coupes: Counterbalanced, automatically locking deck lid, with concealed hinges. Sidewall trim and rubber floor mat. Spare wheel and tire mounted vertically in well at right side. Hold-down spring to retain tools. All Station Wagons have four doors. Extra carrying space provided in 8-passenger Townsman by removable center and rear seats—in 6-passenger Handyman ("One-Fifty" and "Two-Ten" models) by folding rear seat.

Special Features of "Two-Ten" and Bel Air Models with Powerglide

Engine: Compression ratio 7.5 to 1. Horsepower 115 at 3600 r.p.m. Heavier crankshaft. Insert type connecting rod bearings. Full pressure feed lubrication. Aluminum Pistons. Self-adjusting hydraulic valve lifters.

Cooling System: Includes transmission oil cooler.

Transmission: Automatic, hydraulic, new three-element torque converter, with planetary gears for reverse and automatic low. Manual selector for hydraulic control of transmission. Safety switch in starter circuit. Maximum torque converter ratio, 2.1 to 1. Planetary gear ratio 1.82 to 1. Over-all Ratios: Drive, 2.1 to 1. Low and Reverse 3.82 to 1.

Tires: 7.10-15-4 ply rating on Convertibles.

Rear Axle: Ratio, 3.55 to 1.

1954 "Two-Ten" 4-door Sedan

1954 Bel Air Sport Coupe

1954 Bel Air 2-door Sedan

Mr. Bill Rupert, Newport Beach, California

A new wider grill, with five vertical struts on its center bar, extends to a point below the headlights adding to the massive appearance of the front end.

The new winged hood ornament adds a flair to that area.

New heavier-looking bumpers are curved at their ends to add to the forward thrust of the headlights.

A restyled hood emblem is narrower, emphasizing the width of the grill.

The headlight lamps have been recessed slightly, and the inner surface of the bezel now has a decorative appearance.

Wheels remain at 15" diameter, and tires are low pressure 6.70 x 15 4-ply rated (6-ply rating on the Townsman). Although black sidewalls are standard, in 1954, for the first time, every illustration in the Sales Brochure shows the extra-cost whitewall options.

New bumper guards are more massive in appearance than formerly.

The parking light is now located directly beneath the headlamps in a new almost rectangular housing which is faired into the sides of the front fenders.

The one-piece curved windshield introduced on the 1953 models remains unchanged. Optional E-Z-Eye Safety Plate Glass offers tint accompanied by a distinctive green shaded band at the top of the windshield to further reduce glare. The bright metal trim around the glass is omitted on the One-Fifty series.

The inside rear view mirrors are suspended from above the windshield in all models except the Bel Air Sport Coupe in which it is affixed to the top of the instrument panel (above).

All models have the bright metal trim at the belt line. The BEL AIR and the TWO-TEN Series have additional trim at the lower body sill and the sides, the ONE-FIFTY lacks these.

A dual stripe appears on the rear fender of the BEL AIR Series cars only.

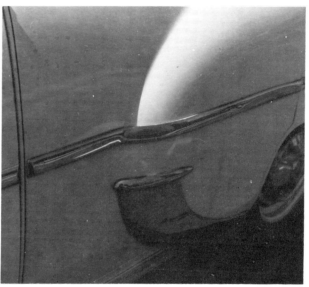

On the TWO-TEN Series, a single stripe appears on the rear fender, and is a continuation of the center body stripe. The ONE-FIFTY Series does not have side trim.

Rear wheel cover panels are standard on the BEL AIR Series only.

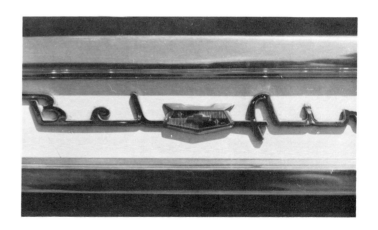

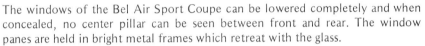

The windows of the Bel Air Sport Coupe can be lowered completely and when concealed, no center pillar can be seen between front and rear. The window panes are held in bright metal frames which retreat with the glass.

Two-door and four-door sedans, and coupes, all have the familiar pillar between the front and rear window panes. The bright metal trim *around* the window is omitted on the One-Fifty Series cars, but all have the lower belt line trim.

The rear license guard is standard on all series but is omitted on the station wagons.

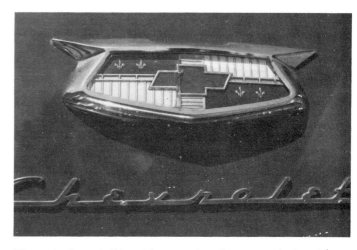

The revised trunk lid emblem matches the one on the hood (page 154). A new script, which differs from that used earlier (page 65) now appears beneath the emblem.

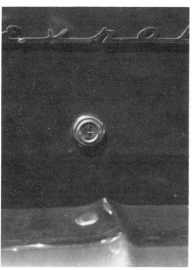

An accessory gas tank lid trim is added.

The tail lamps are revised, losing their familiar reflector button entirely. Beneath the new combined stop-and-tail-light red lens can be seen the white lens for optional back-up lights.

Instrument panel, 1954 Bel Air Sport Coupe

Power Steering is an accessory that is noted by the use of a special steering wheel hub (below).

Two-spoke steering wheels are used with full-circle horn rings on the Bel Air and Two-Ten series. The horn ring is omitted in the One-Fifty Series cars.

Optional Powerglide automatic transmission is available this year on all models.

1946 Fleetline Aerosedan

1947 Fleetmaster Station Wagon

1949 Stylemaster Town Sedan

1950 Bel Air

1952 De Luxe Convertible

1949 Styleline De Luxe Station Wagon (natural wood body)

The sun visors on this and the car on the facing page are accessories.

1953 Bel Air Sport Coupe

1953 Two-Ten Club Coupe

1953 One-Fifty Handyman

1954 Bel Air Sport Coupe

1954 Two-Ten 4-door Sedan

1955 Bel Air No▸

1955 Bel Air Sport Coupe

1955 Bel Air Nomad

1955 Bel Air Convertible

1955 Two-Ten 2-door Sedan

1955 Bel Air Convertible

1955 Bel Air 2-door Sedan

1956 Bel Air Nomad

1956 Bel Air Nomad

1956 Bel Air Sport Coupe

1956 Bel Air Sport Coupe

1957 Bel Air Sport Coupe with optional Fuel Injection system.

1957 Bel Air Townsman 4-door 6-passenger station wagon

1957 Bel Air Nomad 2-door 6-passenger station wagon

1958 Brookwood 6-passenger station wagon.

1958 Bel Air Impala Convertible with accessory continental kit.

1958 Bel Air Impala Sport Coupe

1959 Parkwood 6-passenger station wagon

1959 El Camino

The layout of the 1954 instrument panel is unchanged from 1953 and the 110 mph maximum-reading speedometer is repeated.

Instruments are virtually unchanged from last year. The directional arrows are incorporated into the accessory turn signal kit when it is installed, otherwise are merely decorative.

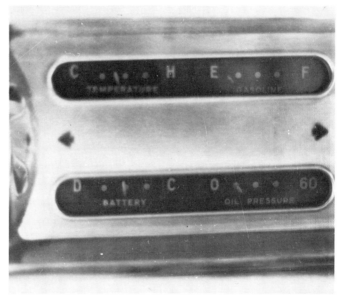

The electric clock is standard in the Bel Air models, an option in the others.

Instrument panel, 1954 Bel Air Sport Coupe

Although its part number is unchanged from the 1953 push-button radio, by 1954, a Chevrolet bow-tie had been added on the tuning dial. A manual tuning radio was also available.

Extolled for its "key-turn" starting, this ignition lock, first used in 1952, later became infamous for its optional unlocked ignition position.

An accessory Air Flow Heater and Defroster incorporates incoming air and is said to "completely change the air in the automobile about every minute". A simpler, recirculating heater was also offered.

The use of a Chevrolet script nameplate on the top center of the instrument panel is continued.

Although the locking package compartment is furnished in all Series, only on the Bel Air and the Two-Ten Series is the interior illuminated.

The practice of using plastic knobs with bright metal inserts on the Bel Air and Two-Ten models is continued (One-Fifty Series cars have plain plastic knobs). Automatic ("Power") windows are offered for the first time, although only on front-door windows of the Bel Air and Two-Ten models. Another newly-introduced option is a power-operated front seat also available in the same two Series only.

CHEVROLET
1955

New Look! New Life (V8 OR 6)! New Everything!

THE BEL AIR 4-DOOR SEDAN

Chevrolet's 3 new engines
put new fun under your foot!

You've got the greatest choice going in the Motoramic Chevrolet! Would you like to boss the new "Turbo-Fire V8" around . . . strictly in charge when the light flashes green . . . calm and confident when the road snakes up a steep grade? (Easy does it—you're handling 162 "horses" with an 8 to 1 compression ratio!) Or would you prefer the equally thrilling performance of one of the two new 6's? There's the new "Blue-Flame 136" teamed with the extra-cost option of a smoother Powerglide. And the new

"Blue-Flame 123" with either the new standard transmission or the extra-cost option of new Touch-Down Overdrive. See why Chevrolet is stealing the thunder from the high-priced cars? It has that high-priced, high-fashion look and everything good that goes with it—power, drives, ride, handling ease, everything. Let your Chevrolet dealer demonstrate how Chevrolet and General Motors have started a whole new age of low-cost motoring! . . . Chevrolet Division of General Motors, Detroit 2, Michigan.

Stealing the thunder from the high-priced cars! **Motoramic** **CHEVROLET**

BEL AIR SERIES
 2-door Sedan
 4-door Sedan
 Sport Coupe
 Convertible
 4-door station wagon
 Nomad

TWO-TEN SERIES
 2-door Sedan
 4-door Sedan
 Del Ray Club Coupe
 2-door station wagon
 4-door station wagon

ONE-FIFTY SERIES
 2-door Sedan
 4-door Sedan
 Utility Sedan
 2-door station wagon

For 1955, Chevrolet could well have advertised "The Name's the Same, but Change is the game", for this was the year for substantial revision.

A distinctive, entirely new style was unveiled. Built on the same 115" wheelbase as previously, Chevrolet manged to reduce the passenger car height and increase the overall length slightly in a restyling that gave a new graceful appearance to the cars. Within the framework of the three-Series line up several changes were made, although some were merely renaming of previous models.

1955 saw the introduction of the Nomad, a new concept which mated a two-door six-passenger luxury sedan with the hauling ability of a station wagon. With unique trim and especially attractive interiors, Chevrolet had made styling modifications to the less-well-remembered Two-Ten 2-door station wagon and produced this memorable new Bel Air model.

Power aides became optionally available in all Series. These included for 1955 Chevrolet's first "factory air", extension of the Power windows option to all windows, new Power Brakes, electric windshield wipers, and the added options of Powerglide, or Overdrive, directional signals, and many more.

With all of this, 1955 still remains best known for its introduction of Chevrolet's new V-8 engine, the first since 1918. With a 265 cubic inch displacement (3.75" bore x 3.0" stroke), the engine featured an 8.0 to 1 compression ratio and was rated at 162 horsepower. It was available with standard three-speed transmission, with or without additional Overdrive, and in a beefed-up version featuring hydraulic lifters and chain-drive timing, in Powerglide installations. Nor was this all; a factory option provided for a larger 4-barrel carburetor and dual exhausts for even greater power.

For those whose affiliation to the long-lived Chevrolet SIX was to be considered, the 1955 Chevrolet also offered two new versions of that engine. The 123 horsepower 235.5 cid version with a 3.56 bore and 3.94 stroke was used with standard transmission with or without Overdrive. Powerglide installations were fitted with a similar engine with hydraulic lifters and a high-lift cam for a rating of 136 horsepower. Both engines used aluminum pistons in place of the cast iron pistons found in Chevrolet's earlier Six Cylinder engines, and both had a new floating-intake oil pump designed to prevent sludge from the bottom of the oil sump from entering the pump.

ENGINEERING SPECIFICATIONS

CAR EXTERIOR DIMENSIONS

Sedans and Coupes: Overall length, 195.6". Overall width, 74.0". Loaded height, 60.5" (Sport Coupe and Convertible, 59.1"). **Station Wagons:** Overall length, 197.1". Overall width, 74.0". Loaded height, 60.8".

POWER PLANT

Engine: 6-cylinder or 8-cylinder, high-compression, valve-in-head engine (in choice of three power teams). Specifications listed below and in center chart.

Pistons: Tin-coated aluminum alloy, with expansion-controlling steel struts, offset pins, and three rings.

Crankshaft: Precision-counterbalanced, forged steel. Rubber-floated harmonic balancer. Alloy iron camshaft.

Bearings: Precision interchangeable steel-backed babbitt crankshaft, camshaft, and connecting rod bearings.

Lubrication: Controlled full-pressure system. Floating oil intake. Crankcase ventilator. Refill, 5 qt. (V8, 4 qt.).

Fuel System: Downdraft carburetion. Automatic choke. Oil-wetted air cleaner. Thermostatic fuel mixture heat control. High-turbulence combustion chambers. 16-gallon tank (17, station wagons) with self-cleaning filter screen. Fuel filler inside of left rear fender, concealed by door.

Exhaust System: 30" reverse-flow muffler with three resonance chambers. Special 24" muffler for Convertible.

Cooling System: Ribbed cellular radiator with pressure cap. 4-blade fan and self-adjusting permanently lubricated water pump. Thermostat and by-pass temperature control. Full-length water jackets around all cylinders. Capacity, 16 qt. (17 qt. with heater).

Electrical System: 12-volt system. 54-plate battery (50 ampere-hour rating at 20 hours). 25-ampere generator, with current and voltage regulators. Solenoid-operated positive-shift starter. All-weather ignition. Automatic centrifugal and vacuum spark control.

Mounting: Dynamically balanced on rubber cushions.

SUSPENSION SYSTEM

Frame and Bumpers: Double-drop box-girder frame (with special X-structure of I-beams in Convertible). Contoured wraparound bumpers, with guards.

Front Suspension: Independent coil spring suspension, with coaxial life-sealed double-acting shock absorbers. Self-adjusting spherical-joint steering knuckles with non-metallic bearings. Four lubrication fittings.

Rear Suspension: Semi-elliptic leaf springs, 58" long by 2" wide. Lubrication-eliminating leaf inserts. Outrigger mounting, with compression shackles. Diagonally mounted life-sealed double-acting shock absorbers.

Wheels and Tires: Short-spoke steel disk wheels; 5" rims. Full wheel disks on Bel Air models; hub caps on others. 6.70-15-4 p.r. extra-low-pressure tubeless tires. Wheelbase, 115". Front tread, 58". Rear tread, 58.8".

CONTROLS

Brakes: Hydraulic, self-energizing, with bonded linings. 11" dia. drums with cast alloy iron braking surfaces. Braking dive controlled by car suspension system. Mechanical actuation of rear brakes for parking.

Steering: Recirculating ball-nut steering gear; ratio 20 to 1. Relay type linkage. Overall ratio, 25.7 to 1.

Driving Controls: 18" steering wheel (3-spoke on Bel Air models; 2-spoke on others). Full-circle horn ring on Bel Air and "Two-Ten" models; horn button on "One-Fifty" models. Transmission and direction signal* control levers, with mechanism inside steering column. Parking brake T-handle at left of steering column. Suspended brake and clutch pedals. Treadle accelerator. Foot-controlled headlight-beam switch. Light switch. Key-turn starter and ignition lock switch. Windshield wiper and ventilation controls.

Instruments: Speedometer. Fuel gauge. Heat indicator. Generator charge, oil pressure, and country beam warning lights. Direction signal* arrows. Adjustable indirect instrument lighting. Lighted automatic transmission* selector indicator on instrument panel.

Vision Aids: Two windshield wipers. Full-width defrosting. Inside mirror. Two sun shades (one, "One-Fifty" models).

Driving Lights: Sealed beam headlights, protected by dual circuit breakers. Parking lights. Tail and stop light units, with red reflex buttons. Dual rear license lights.

BODY CONSTRUCTION

Structure: Welded steel. Turret top with central bow (except Convertible). Full-length floor. Double-walled cowl. Unitized sides and rear fenders. Lacquer finish.

Closures: Rear-opening double-walled doors: Concealed hinges; swing-out type front door hinges. Door checks. Rotary locks. Pushbutton outside handles; lever inside controls. Button-on-sill latches, with rear door safety adjustment. Aluminum sill plates. Two-panel sedan and coupe deck lid: Concealed counterbalancing hinges, key release, lift handle, slam latch. Extra-low trunk sill. Box-section station wagon lift gate: Concealed hinges, self-latching supports, wedge lock. Double-walled station wagon tail gate: Exposed hinges, support cables with re-wind springs, slam latches operated by outside T-handle. Key locks for both front doors, deck lid or end gates. Front-opening hood: Counterbalancing hinges, slam latch with safety catch. Convertible folding fabric top: Zippered-in rear curtain with vinyl plastic window, vinyl boot, hydraulic operating mechanism.

Insulation: Thorough sealing and insulation. Extra top sound deadener in Bel Air and "Two-Ten" models.

Front Ventilation: High-level air intake in top of cowl; individually controlled outlets in cowl side panels.

Mounting: Rubber cushioned (except Convertible). Stabilized mounting of front fenders, hood and radiator.

POWER TEAMS	CONVENTIONAL		OVERDRIVE		AUTOMATIC	
Engine Size	123-hp Six 235.5 cu. in. displacement. 3.56" bore, 3.94" stroke. 7.5 to 1 compression ratio.	162-hp V8 265.0 cu. in. displacement. 3.75" bore, 3.0" stroke. 8.0 to 1 compression ratio.	123-hp Six 235.5 cu. in. displacement. 3.56" bore, 3.94" stroke. 7.5 to 1 compression ratio.	162-hp V8 265.0 cu. in. displacement. 3.75" bore, 3.0" stroke. 8.0 to 1 compression ratio.	136-hp Six 235.5 cu. in. displacement. 3.56" bore, 3.94" stroke. 7.5 to 1 compression ratio.	162-hp V8 265.0 cu. in. displacement. 3.75" bore, 3.0" stroke. 8.0 to 1 compression ratio.
Engine Special Features	Concentric carburetor. 4-bearing crankshaft. Gear drive timing.	Dual carburetor. 5-bearing crankshaft. Chain drive timing.	Concentric carburetor. 4-bearing crankshaft. Gear drive timing.	Dual carburetor. 5-bearing crankshaft. Chain drive timing.	Concentric carburetor. 4-bearing crankshaft. High-lift camshaft. Gear drive timing. Hydraulic valve lifters.	Dual carburetor. 5-bearing crankshaft. Chain drive timing. Hydraulic valve lifters.
Clutch	9½" dia.	10" dia.	9½" dia.	10" dia.		
	Diaphragm spring type. Life-lubricated throwout bearing. Strap drive.					
Transmission	Heavy-Duty Transmission 3-speed, synchro-mesh, selective gear transmission, with gearshift lever on steering column. Gear Ratios: First . . . . . . 2.94 to 1 Second . . . . . . 1.68 to 1 Third . . . . . . 1.00 to 1 Reverse . . . . . . 2.94 to 1		Heavy-Duty Transmission plus Overdrive* 3-pinion, planetary gear overdrive, providing automatic fourth speed; gear ratio, 0.71 to 1. Accelerator control: Electric cut-in, through releasing treadle, at approx. 25 mph.; down-shift to direct drive by pressing treadle to floor. Pull-out knob locks out overdrive.		Automatic Transmission* Hydraulic, 3-element torque converter, with planetary gears for reverse and automatic low. Selector lever on steering column. Safety switch in starter circuit. Oil cooler integrated with engine cooling system. Maximum torque converter ratio, 2.1 to 1. Planetary gear ratio, 1.82 to 1. Maximum overall ratio, 3.82 to 1.	
Rear Axle	Semi-floating, with hypoid gears. One-piece "banjo" housing. Hotchkiss drive.					
	3.70 to 1 ratio		4.11 to 1 ratio		3.55 to 1 ratio	

BODY EQUIPMENT

Windows: Polished safety plate glass in windshield and all windows. Windshield: One-piece wraparound; vertical pillars. Door windows: Crank-down. Crank-operated front door ventipanes. Rear quarter windows: Crank down (2-door sedans, coupes). Stationary (4-door sedans, Utility Sedan). Wraparound stationary (station wagons) with crank-down front sections ("Two-Ten" 2-door model). Rear window: Wraparound (sedans, coupes except Convertible). Curved (station wagons).

Seats: Full-width; all-steel frames with S-wire springs. Front seat: Solid back (4-door models); split center-fold back (2-door models). Foam rubber cushion (Bel Air and "Two-Ten" models). Inclined-plane seat adjustment. Rear seat: Foam rubber cushion (Bel Air and "Two-Ten" sedans, coupes). Folding seat (station wagons).

Upholstery and Trim: All vinyl (Convertible, Club Coupe, "Two-Ten" and "One-Fifty" station wagons), combinations of pattern cloth, gabardine, vinyl (others). Chrome front seat and side wall moldings (Bel Air and "Two-Ten" models); windshield top and side molding (Convertible); roof bows (Sport Coupe).

Floor Coverings: Carpet (Bel Air sedans, coupes; Club Coupe). Rubber mats (others), also sedan and coupe trunk, Utility Sedan load space. Linoleum on platform, tail gate, and surface of folded rear seat (station wagons).

Appointments: Wraparound instrument panel with instrument cluster in front of driver, matching radio grille, and central glove compartment with key lock. Automatic glove compartment light, ash receptacle, and cigarette lighter (Bel Air and "Two-Ten" models) and electric clock (Bel Air models). Four arm rests (Bel Air and "Two-Ten" models, except two in station wagons). Two rear seat ash receptacles (Bel Air and "Two-Ten" 2-door models; one, Bel Air and "Two-Ten" 4-door sedans). Two assist straps (Bel Air and "Two-Ten" 2-door sedans, Club Coupe). Package shelf (sedans, coupes except Convertible).

Lights: Central dome light (sedans, Club Coupe, station wagons). Two rear corner lights (Sport Coupe). Two courtesy lights under instrument panel (Convertible). Manual control by light switch on instrument panel. Automatic switches at all doors (Bel Air models, "Two-Ten" 2-door models); at front doors ("Two-Ten" 4-door models).

Exterior Chrome: Hood ornament, hood and rear emblems, light bezels, radiator grille, bumpers, ventipane frames, handles, hub caps or wheel disks (all models). "V" on rear fenders (V8 models). Windshield, window sill, rear side, and sash moldings ("Two-Ten" models). Windshield and side window moldings; rear window reveal (except Convertible); windshield pillar moldings; front, sash, and rear side moldings (Bel Air models). Special top and belt moldings, and winged spears replacing sash moldings (Bel Air and "Two-Ten" station wagons).

FACTORY-INSTALLED OPTIONAL EQUIPMENT*

Four-barrel carburetor and dual exhaust system for V8 engines. Overdrive. Automatic transmission, in combination with either 6-cylinder engine or V8 engine. Low-pedal vacuum-power brakes. Hydraulic power steering. Direction signals. Electric windshield wipers. Tinted safety plate glass. Electric-power window lifts. Electric-power front seat adjustment. Heater and defroster. Air conditioner. Whitewall tires.

1955

1955 Bel Air Convertible

1955 Two-Ten 2-door Sedan

1955 Bel Air Sport Coupe

Jon Guilmet, San Diego, California

1955 Bel Air 2-door Sedan

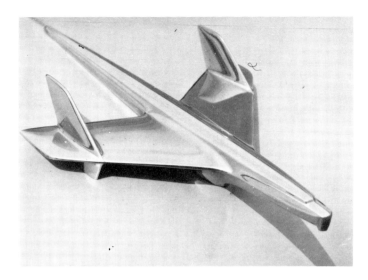

A new hood ornament having a longer look than the 1953 style (page 154) now appears.

These are accessory bumper tips, added to give a more massive appearance.

A new longer, and narrower, hood ornament now appears.

The 1955 "egg crate" grill is a departure from the "toothed" grill of recent years.

The clean, uncluttered look of the 1955 Chevrolet results largely from the use of a new grill and front bumper.

The new, more massive bumpers require a new guard.

This grill guard is an accessory which replaces the two standard bumper guards as well.

This Chevrolet script appears on the front fenders of the Two-Ten and the One-Fifty Series cars only.

New wrap-around front bumpers sweep well around the front corners to the wheel opening.

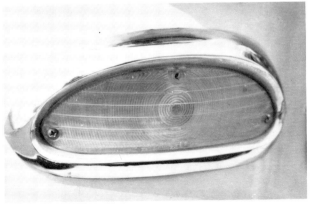

New tear-drop shaped parking lamps appear below the headlights in a simplified housing exposing a parting line in the fender side panel.

Newly formed fenders have a protruding "brow" over the headlamps.

A chromed headlight bezel emphasizes the visor-like effect of the fenders.

The entire front corner of the car has been re-styled to emphasize the forward thrust of the vehicle.

Although the fenders all have the characteristic "crease", only on the Bel Air series does the added front trim strip appear. Wheel size remains at 15 inches, tires are 6.70 x 15 as previously.

A new "Sweep-Sight Windshield" curves around at the ends. The bright metal trim around the glass is again omitted on the One-Fifty models.

With vertical windshield pillars, the vent windows assume a new rectangular shape.

The inside rear view mirrow is now suspended from above the windhsield on all models, including the Sport Coupe.

Just forward of the windshield, a grill now appears, the high-level entry point for ventilating air.

The ends of the new wrap-around windshield curve gracefully around to meet near-vertical pillars.

An added wind and rain deflector above the front windows of the Bel Air Sport Coupe is hinged and triggered to flip up (left) when the door is opened.

With windows lowered, the Bel Air Sport Coupe passengers have an unobstructed view.

Metal-framed windows of the Bel Air Sport Coupe can be lowered into the body.

The TWO-TEN Series has, in addition to the simulated air scoop of the Bel Air, a single stripe on its rear fenders. The ONE-FIFTY cars are devoid of such ornamentation.

The rear fenders of the BEL AIR Series cars have a dual stripe trim and other distinctive features (below).

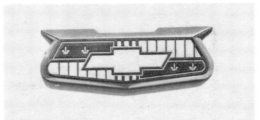

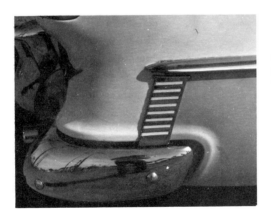

Added trim characteristics of the Bel Air Series cars are the nameplate and side emblem, and the trim plate just above the rear bumper tips.

Wheel cover panels, long a characteristics of the Bel Air Series, are deleted with the advent of the 1955 model.

New outside door handles with oval push-buttons replace the earlier round-button style (page 157).

A dress-up accessory trim plate behind the door handle helps to protect the door paint.

A return to the separate outside door lock in place of the earlier style (page 157) adds a keylock below the front door handles.

A trim strip, simulating an air scoop, is placed at the hip line of the Bel Air and the Two-Ten series cars.

A handsome new ornamental emblem appears on the rear deck lid as well as the hood.

Restyled rear bumper guards contain lamps to illuminate the license plate.

A rubber mat appears in the large luggage compartment. The counter-balanced lid hinges ease lifting.

The separate key lock releases the rear deck lid latch.

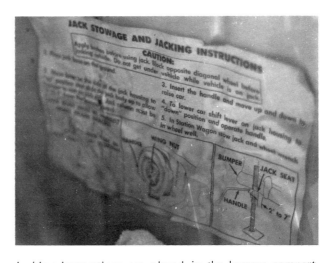

Jacking instructions are placed in the luggage compartment inside the right rear fender.

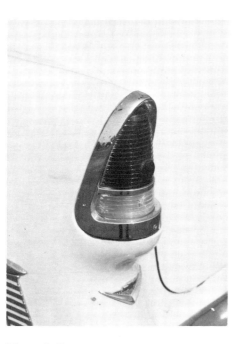

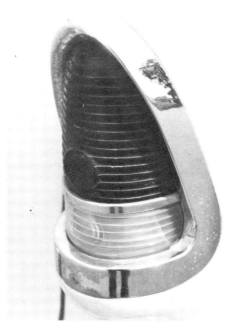

An entirely new, somewhat angular, tail light now appears, but back-up lights and directional signals remain extra cost options.

The tail light assembly is designed as a visible part of the rear fender into which it fits.

This emblem appears under the tail lights (upper left) only on those cars in which the V-8 engine is installed.

The gas tank filler tube is located under a flap in the left rear fender. Unlike past installations, (page 159), the flap is now hinged at its forward edge.

The factory-installed Plus Power Package option included a four-barrel carburetor and dual exhausts on the V-8 engine. Dress-up, "Power Pack" tips were also provided on the exhaust pipes (below).

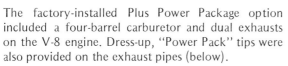

Standard Chevrolet exhaust pipe is oval-tipped.

The 1955 Bel Air Convertible interior is inviting and access to the rear seat is adequate. (The current owner has installed protective vinyl slip covers.)

The folding top of the Convertible is power-operated.

A distinctive two-tone pattern is used on the seats of the Convertible.

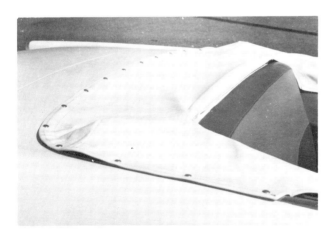

A boot is furnished to protect the folded top of the Convertible.

The front seats of all models are adjustable and move in an inclined track which raises seat as it moves forward. A power-operated seat is available as an option, or seat may be manually adjusted by releasing knob (left).

Interior view, 1955 Bel Air Convertible

The basic Bel Air instrument panel, like the others, does not include a radio. This is an extra-cost accessory.

This unique black knob is used on both standard and automatic transmission shift levers.

Reversing previous installations, the Bel Air series is furnished with a special *three*-spoke steering wheel with a full-circle horn blowing ring. Two-spoke steering wheels are used on the Two-Ten and One-Fifty cars, but the horn ring only appears in the Two-Ten.

Steering wheel hubs bear decorative emblems. This one signifies a six-cylinder engine car. A "V" emblem (page 226) is used on eight cylinder cars.

Direction signals are a factory option at extra cost.

A new 12-volt electric system appeared in the 1955 models ending the use of the former 6-volt system. Although functionally similar, there is therefore no interchangeability between 1955 and earlier electric components such as instruments, radio, clock, lamp bulbs, starter, generator, etc.

Optional Powerglide brings a visible indicator at the base of the speedometer. Standard transmission installations are fitted with a blanking plate at this point (left).

An entirely new speedometer is housed beneath a hood formed in the surface of the instrument panel.

Round warning lights (above and left) replace the gauges and illuminate to warn of Low Oil Pressure (above) or Battery Discharge.

New knobs are used on the instrument panel.

Functionally unchanged, the ignition switch is flanked by a standard blanking plate (above) or optional heater controls (below). Beneath the switch (below) can be seen the Overdrive control.

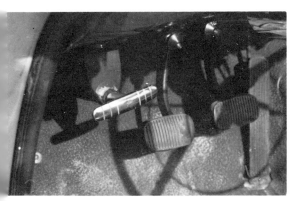

The new T-handle parking brake is moved to the left side, and foot pedals are now suspended. (compare page 160.)

Function knobs on the 1955 instrument panel are fitted with legible eschutcheon plates.

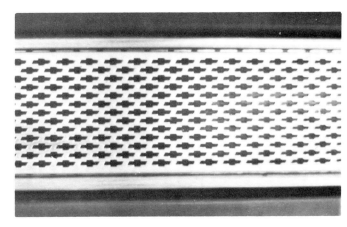

The Chevrolet bow-tie emblem is repeated endlessly in a pattern pierced in the instrument panel trim.

The radio blanking plate, furnished when that accessory is not purchased, matches the bow tie trim. Beneath it can be seen the package compartment which has been placed at the center of the instrument panel.

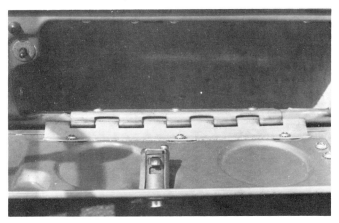

The locking package compartment has interior lighting (in the Bel Air and Two-Ten models only) operated by the switch seen at the upper left.

The electric clock is standard in Bel Air models only, but available as an option in the others. Its speed is adjusted by a screw placed between the numerals at the twelve o'clock position.

Available for the first time, in 1955, is this signal-seeking Wonder Bar push-button radio. A manual tuning economy model as well as a conventional push button version were also offered.

The radio speaker is installed behind this standard grill at the right side of the instrument panel. The decorative Bel Air nameplate is replaced by a Chevrolet script (below) on the Two-Ten and One-Fifty models.

An antenna for the accessory radio is installed on the right front fender.

When the electric clock option is not installed in the Two-Ten or One-Fifty models, a blanking plate is furnished.

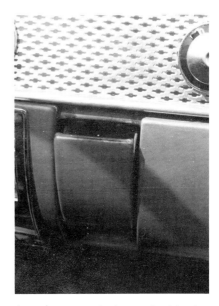

The optional Ventilating Heater and Defroster controls replace a standard blanking panel at the bottom of the instrument panel. An alternate economy Recirculating Heater control head also fits this space.

An ash receptacle is standard in the Bel Air Two-Ten Series, but is not furnished in the One-Fifty models.

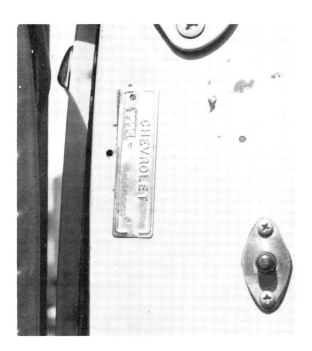

Inside door locks are standard and protrude through the sill.

The use of a serial number plate on the left front door jamb is continued. The automatic switch for the interior lights is standard on all doors of the Bel Air Series cars and the front doors only in the Two-Ten models. It is not furnished on the One-Fifty Models.

The upholstery panels of the Bel Air Series are distinctively done in two-tone vinyl with bright metal trim strips and moulded-in arm rests on the front doors.

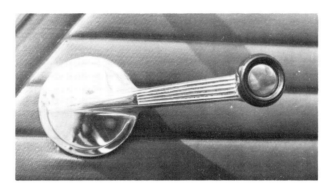

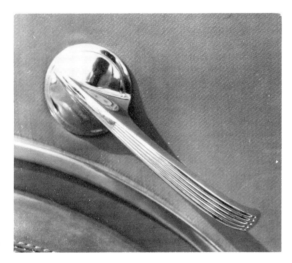

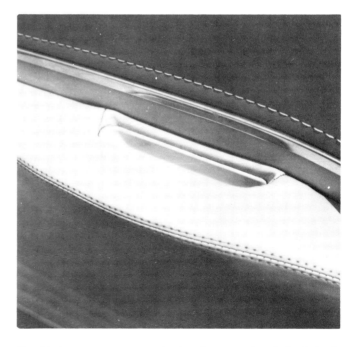

Moulded arm rests appear in the door panels of the Bel Air models. Conventional unitized arm rests are furnished in the front doors of the Two-Ten models and all station wagons. No arm rests are provided in the economy One-Fifty models.

Hoods are front-opening on all models.

Running from the rear left corner of the V-8 manifold is a semi-flexible copper tube connected to a temperature sensing probe. Used only on the 1955 V-8, the "mechanical" manifold was modified in 1956 to accept an electrical sensor and the copper tube deleted.

This is a factory accessory oil filter. The 1955 block had no other provision for filtering the oil.

A factory-installed option, the new Plus-Power Package boosts the standard V-8 horsepower from 162 to 180 with dual exhausts, four-barrel carburetor, etc.

Two steel valve covers bearing the Chevrolet name are used on the new V-8 engines.

A new oil-bath air cleaner is employed on the new V-8.

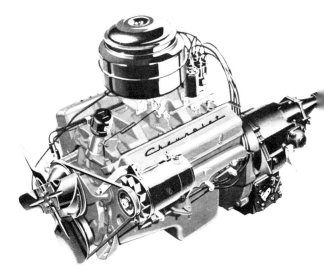

1955 Chevrolet 162 horsepower V-8 engine.

Two Sixes are available. The standard engine, with Synchro-Mesh transmission, is rated at 123 horspower. The Power-glide version with the high-lift cam, hydraulic lifters, and other changes, is rated at 136 hp.

Compared to the crowded V-8 engine, the six-cylinder 1955 engine seems small for the available space.

The 123 H.P. SIX shown here is externally identical to the 136 horsepower version used with Powerglide installations.

Dual horns are mounted ahead of the radiator.

1955 Chevrolet 123 horsepower SIX

In an unusual illustration from the 1955 Sales Folder, Chevrolet's new 1955 chassis can be viewed easily.

1955 Nomad

Derived from a one-off "dream car" first shown at the GM Motorama early in 1954, the attractive new 1955 Bel Air Nomad was a luxurious 2-door, 6-passenger station wagon. With unique mechanical features including a rear window that wrapped around to its corner post, the model featured a rear seat that could be folded to increase cargo space.

The Nomad was not Chevrolet's only 2-door 1955 station wagon. In addition there was offered a Two-Ten and a One-Fifty model, each with descending standard trim and upholstery. However, the Nomad is remembered best because despite unmistakably good looks, it failed to create a place for itself. The Nomad was to be continued for only two more years and then discontinued.

1955 Bel Air Nomad

1955 Bel Air Nomad featuring optional two-tone paint.

Mr. Earl Bryan, Bellflower, California

1955 Nomad

Unique to the Nomad are the chromed trim pieces fitted over the headlamp housing.

Nomad, the highest priced model of Chevrolet's line, was often furnished with added dress-up items. The front grill guard is one such an accessory.

On the Nomad only, a simple side trim stripe starting at the headlamps, continues to the rear edge of the door. The trim on the fender at the rear of the front wheel is dress-up accessory.

The all-steel roof of the Nomad station wagon has distinctive strengthening "ribs" towards its rear.

The forward portion of the roof is smooth. Decorative transverse "ribs" run over the side above the quarter windows.

This graceful center pillar is unique to the Nomad.

The front windows curve at their trailing edge to match the curve of the pillar.

The forward portion of the rear quarter window slides open for ventilation.

207

1955 Nomad

The Nomad shares the tail light design of the other 1955 models.

The Nomad appears longer than it actually is due to the extension of the rear fenders (and tail lights) beyond the tailgate.

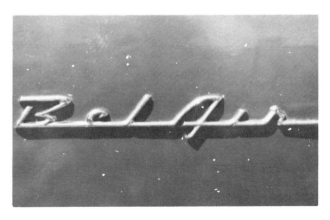

The side trim includes the Bel Air script and familiar emblem (upper left).

The rear end of the Nomad is unique in appearance. Featuring wraparound windows, narrow pillars, emphatic stripes on the tailgate, it is unmistakable.

Seven bright metal trim stripes are used on Nomad models only.

The Nomad name appears on the tailgate just above the locking handle.

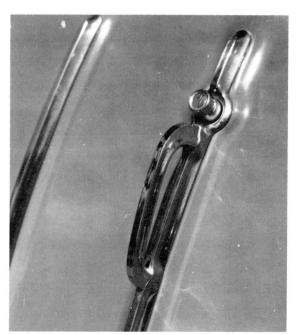

The tailgate latch is released by depressing the lockable push button. The back window ("lift gate") is hinged at its top and provided with telescoping supports (page 235).

1955 Nomad

A split back front seat is hinged to allow access to the rear bench seat.

The headliner of the Nomad is held in place by seven chromed metal bows, five of which may be seen in this view.

The second (rear) seat of the Nomad, like other 2-door station wagons, can be folded for added cargo, but in this position provides adequate seating for three passengers.

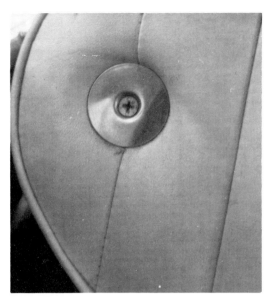

Special hardware at the tip of the folding rear seat back secures a latching mechanism.

A tire pressure decal is placed on the edge of the door.

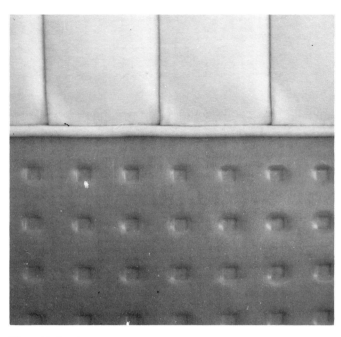

The distinctive Nomad vinyl waffle pattern upholstery is found in other models as well, notably the 1956/57 Corvettes.

The bottom of the Nomad doors is protected with patterned metal scuff plates.

The narrow back pillars and abundantly curved quarter glass windows are distinctive to the Nomad.

Some 1955
Accessories

Among the most enduring of the extra-cost options is
Air Conditioning, a feature first offered in the 1955 model.
Engineered into the instrument panel, not merely suspended beneath it, it has continued to be one of the most popular luxury accessories.

The accessory Air Conditioner is fully installed behind
the instrument panel and in the engine compartment. Its
only evidence is the two adjustable vents placed at the ends
of the instrument panel, and the control head which replaces the standard blanking plate (page 197).

**Some 1955
Accessories**

Non-Glare Rear View Mirror

Headlamp Dress-up Trim

Front Grill Guard

Lower Body Side Stripe

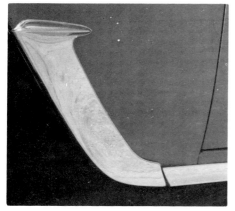

Fender Dress-up Trim

Gas Tank Door Trim

Locking Gas Cap

Front and Rear Bumper Tips

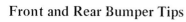

Exhaust Deflector

Chevrolet

offering a bigger, brighter choice than ever!

BEL AIR SERIES

2-door Sedan
4-door Sedan
Sport Sedan   (4-door hardtop)
Sport Coupe   (2-door hardtop)
Convertible
Beauville   (4-door, 9-passenger station wagon)
Nomad

TWO-TEN SERIES

2-door Sedan
4-door Sedan
Sport Sedan   (4-door hardtop)
Sport Coupe   (2 door hardtop)
Delray Club Coupe
Beauville   (4-door, 9-passenger station wagon)
Townsman   (4-door, 6-passenger station wagon)
Handyman   (2-door, 6 passenger station wagon)

ONE-FIFTY SERIES

2-door Sedan
4-door Sedan
Utility Sedan   (3-passenger business sedan)
Handyman   (2-door, 6 passengstation wagon)

Loves to go...*and looks it !*
The '56 Chevrolet

The Bel Air Sport Sedan is one of two new Chevrolet 4-door hardtops. All 19 new models feature Body by Fisher.

*It's got frisky new power...V8 or 6...
to make the going sweeter and the passing safer. It's
agile...quick...solid and sure on the road!*

This, you remember, is the car that set a new record for the Pikes Peak run. And the car that can take that tough and twisting climb in record time is bound to make *your* driving safer and more fun.

Curve ahead? You level through it with a wonderful nailed-to-the-road feeling of stability. Chevrolet's special suspension and springing see to that.

Slow car ahead? You whisk around it and back in line in seconds. Chevrolet's new high-compression power—ranging from the new "Blue-Flame 140" Six up to 225 h.p. in the new Corvette V8 engine, available at extra cost—handles that.

Quick stop called for? Nudge those oversize brakes and relax. Chevrolet's exclusive Anti-Dive braking brings you to a smooth, *heads-up* halt.

No doubt about it, this bold beauty was made for the road. Like to try it? Just see your Chevrolet dealer.... Chevrolet Division of General Motors, Detroit 2, Michigan.

THE HOT ONE'S EVEN HOTTER

CHEVROLET

1956 was a "mark time" year for Chevrolet. Having leap-frogged with its 1955 model they reserved their right to move slowly with added change.

Built on the same 115" chassis used in 1955, the new models received a grill restyle and changes in the side trim including newly-shaped wheel cut-outs in the fenders which added to an appearance of motion even at standstill.

A new model, the Sport Sedan, was introduced in both the Bel Air and also the Two-Ten Series. A 4-door sedan with disappearing center posts and wrap-around rear window, the model was a companion to the very popular Sport Coupe in both appearance and intent. Not yet referred to as a "hardtop" or "hardtop convertible", the style was nevertheless unique. However, although it greatly resembled the Sport Coupe, the Sport Sedan was never to receive the popularity of the former.

Under the hood, engine choice was again available in either a six, or the more popular eight-cylinder engine. Only one version of the Six was available, a high 8.0 to 1 compression ratio 140 horsepower model, but the V-8 was offered in a basic 162 hp version which varied up to 225 horsepower when equipped with the factory "Corvette V-8" package which featured a 9.25:1 compression ratio, dual 4-barrel carburetors, high-lift camshaft, dual exhausts, and high-speed mechanical lifters.

Despite this reference to their Corvette, Chevrolet's sales literature for 1956 again failed to illustrate *their new sports car. Introduced as an intended trend-setter for the whole line, Corvette had so far failed to make any great impressions and would not for another year appear as an integral part of the overall Chevrolet passenger car line.*

ENGINEERING SPECIFICATIONS

CAR EXTERIOR DIMENSIONS

Sedans and Coupes: Overall length, 197.5". Overall width, 74.0". Loaded height, 60.5" (Sport Coupe, Sport Sedan, and Convertible, 59.1"). **Station Wagons:** Overall length, 200.8". Overall width, 74.0". Loaded height, 60.8".

POWER PLANT

Engine: 6 cylinder or 8 cylinder, high-compression, valve in head engine with h.p. ranging up to 225. Specifications listed below and in center chart.

Pistons: Tin-coated aluminum alloy, with expansion controlling steel struts, offset pins, three rings.

Crankshaft: Precision-counterbalanced, forged steel. Harmonic balancer. Alloy iron camshaft.

Bearings: Precision replaceable steel-backed babbitt (crankshaft, and connecting rods).

Lubrication: Controlled full-pressure system. Fixed oil intake. Oil Filter*. Refill, 5 qt. (V8, 4 qt.).

Fuel System: Downdraft carburetion. Automatic choke. Air cleaner. Thermostatic fuel mixture heat control. High-turbulence combustion chambers. 16-gallon tank (17, station wagons) with filter screen in tank. Fuel filler concealed by left tail light.

Exhaust System: 30" reverse-flow muffler with three resonance chambers. Special 24" muffler for Convertible. Super Turbo-Fire V8 and Corvette V8 have full dual exhaust system.

Cooling System: Ribbed cellular radiator with pressure cap. 4-blade fan and life-lubricated water pump. Thermostat and by-pass temperature control. Full-length water jackets around all cylinders. Capacity, 16 qt. (17 qt. with heater).

Electrical System: 12-volt system. 54-plate battery (53 ampere-hour rating at 20 hours). 25-ampere generator, with current and voltage regulators. Solenoid-actuated positive-shift starter. All-weather ignition. Automatic centrifugal and vacuum spark control.

Mounting: Balanced on rubber cushions.

SUSPENSION SYSTEM

Frame and Bumpers: Double-drop box-girder frame (special X-structure of I-beams in Convertible). Contoured wraparound bumpers, with guards.

Front Suspension: Independent coil spring suspension, with coaxial life-sealed double-acting shock absorbers. Self-adjusting spherical-joint steering knuckles with non-metallic bearings. Four lubrication fittings.

Rear Suspension: Semi-elliptic leaf springs, 58" by 2". Lubrication-eliminating leaf inserts. Outrigger mounting, with compression shackles. Diagonally mounted life-sealed double-acting shock absorbers.

Wheels and Tires: Steel disk wheels; 5" rims. Full wheel disks on Bel Air models; hub caps on others. 6.70-15-4 p.r. extra-low-pressure tubeless tires. 6.70-15-6 p.r. on nine passenger station wagons. Wheelbase, 115". Front tread, 58". Rear tread, 58.8".

CONTROLS

Brakes: Hydraulic, self-energizing, with bonded linings. 11" dia. drums with cast alloy iron braking surfaces. Braking dive controlled by suspension. Mechanical actuation of rear brakes for parking.

Steering: Recirculating ball-nut steering gear; ratio 20 to 1. Relay type linkage. Overall ratio, 25.7 to 1.

Driving Controls: 18" steering wheel (3-spoke on Bel Air models; 2-spoke on others). Full-circle horn ring on Bel Air and "Two-Ten" models; horn button on "One-Fifty" models. Transmission and direction signal control levers, with mechanism inside steering column. Parking brake T-handle at left of steering column. Suspended brake and clutch pedals. Treadle accelerator. Foot-controlled headlight beam switch. Light switch. Key-turn starter and ignition lock switch. Windshield wiper and ventilation controls.

Instruments: Speedometer. Fuel gauge. Heat indicator. Generator charge, oil pressure, and country beam warning lights. Direction signal arrows. Adjustable indirect instrument lighting. Lighted automatic transmission selector indicator on instrument panel.

Vision Aids: Two windshield wipers. Full-width defrosting. Inside mirror. Two sun shades (one, "One-Fifty" models).

Driving Lights: Precision-aimed sealed beam headlights, protected by dual circuit breakers. Parking lights. Tail and stop light units, with red reflex buttons. Dual rear license lights.

BODY CONSTRUCTION

Structure: Welded steel. Turret top with central bow (except Convertible). Station wagons (except Nomad) have two roof bows. Full-length floor. Double-walled cowl. Unitized sides and rear fenders. Lacquer finish.

Closures: Rear-opening double-walled doors: Concealed hinges; swing-out type front door hinges. Door checks. Safety type rotary locks. Pushbutton outside handles; lever inside controls. Button-on-sill locks, with rear door safety adjustment. Aluminum sill plates. Two-panel sedan and coupe deck lid: Concealed torque-rod counterbalancing hinges, key release, lift handle, slam latch. Extra-low trunk sill. Box-section station wagon lift gate: Concealed hinges, self-latching supports, wedge lock. Double-walled station wagon tail gate: Exposed hinges, support cables with re-wind springs, slam latches operated by outside T-handle. Key locks for both front doors, deck lid or end gates. Front-opening hood: Counterbalancing hinges, slam latch with safety catch. Convertible folding fabric top: Zippered-in rear curtain with vinyl plastic window, vinyl boot, hydraulic operating mechanism.

Insulation: Thorough sealing and insulation.

Front Ventilation: High-level air intake in top of cowl; individually controlled outlets in cowl sides.

Mounting: Rubber cushioned (except Convertible). Stabilized front end mounting.

BODY EQUIPMENT

Windows: High quality safety glass in windshield and all windows. Windshield: One-piece panoramic, vertical pillars. Door windows: Crank-down. Crank-operated front door ventipanes. Rear quarter windows: Crank-down (2-door sedans, coupes). Stationary (4-door sedans, Utility Sedan). Wrap-around stationary (station wagons) with movable front sections (Bel Air and "Two-Ten" 2-door models). Rear window: Wraparound (sedans, coupes except Convertible). Curved (station wagons).

Seats: Full-width; steel frames with S-wire springs. Front seat: Solid back (4-door models); split center-fold back (2-door models). Foam rubber cushion (Bel Air and "Two-Ten" models). Inclined-plane seat adjustment. Rear seat: Foam rubber cushion (Bel Air sedans, coupes and Nomad). Folding seat (six-passenger station wagons). Nine-passenger station wagon: Folding center seat with off-center divided back, removable rear seat.

Upholstery and Trim: All vinyl (Convertible, Club Coupe, "Two-Ten" and "One-Fifty" station wagons), combinations of pattern cloth and vinyl (others). Chrome front seat and side wall moldings (Bel Air and "Two-Ten" models); windshield top and side molding (Convertible). Vinyl headlining (Bel Air Sport Coupe, Sport Sedan, Nomad).

Floor Coverings: Carpet (Bel Air sedans, coupes, Nomad; "Two-Ten" Club Coupe). Rubber mats (others), also sedan and coupe trunk, Utility Sedan load space. Linoleum on platform, tail gate, and surface of folded rear seat (station wagons).

Appointments: Wraparound instrument panel with instrument cluster in front of driver, matching radio grille, ashtray and central glove compartment with key lock. Automatic glove compartment light, ashtray on instrument panel on all jobs, and cigarette lighter (Bel Air and "Two-Ten" models) and electric clock (Bel Air models). Four arm rests (Bel Air and "Two-Ten" models, except two in station wagons). Two rear seat ash receptacles (Bel Air and "Two-Ten" 2-door models; one, Bel Air and "Two-Ten" 4-door sedans). Two assist straps (Bel Air and "Two-Ten" 2-door sedans, Club Coupe). Package shelf (sedans, coupes except Convertible).

Lights: Central dome light. Two courtesy lights under instrument panel (Convertible), two lights in Nomad. Manual switch on instrument panel. Automatic switches at all doors (Bel Air models); at front doors ("Two-Ten" models).

Exterior Chrome: Hood ornament, hood and rear emblems, light bezels, grille, bumpers, ventipane frames, handles, hub caps or wheel disks. "V" on hood and rear deck (V8 models). V's on Nomad rear fenders. Windshield, rear window, side, and sash moldings ("Two-Ten" and "One-Fifty" models), window sill ("Two-Ten" models). Windshield and side window moldings; rear window reveal (except Convertible); windshield pillar moldings; sash and double side moldings (Bel Air models). Special top and belt moldings (Bel Air and "Two-Ten" station wagons)

FACTORY-INSTALLED OPTIONAL EQUIPMENT*

Overdrive. Automatic transmission. Heavy-duty oil bath air cleaner (all 6-cylinder models). Heavy-duty clutch. Low-pedal vacuum-power brakes. Hydraulic power steering. Electric windshield wipers. Tinted safety glass. Electric-power window lifts. Electric-power front seat adjustment. Heater and defroster. Air conditioner. Whitewall tires. Six ply tires. Heavy-duty rear springs.

POWER TEAMS	CONVENTIONAL	OVERDRIVE	AUTOMATIC
Blue-Flame 140	Valve-in-head 140-h.p. Six-cylinder engine. 235.5 cubic inch displacement. 3.56" bore, 3.94" stroke, 8.0 to 1 compression ratio. Concentric carburetor, 4-bearing crankshaft, gear-drive timing, hydraulic valve lifters.		
Turbo-Fire V8	Valve-in-head 162-h.p. (170-h.p. with Powerglide) V8 engine. 265 cubic inch displacement. 3.75" bore, 3.0" stroke, 8.0 to 1 compression ratio. Two-barrel carburetor. 5-bearing crankshaft, chain-drive timing, hydraulic valve lifters. Heavy-duty oil-bath air cleaner.		
Super Turbo-Fire V8	Valve-in-head 205-h.p. V8 engine. 265 cubic inch displacement. 3.75" bore, 3.0" stroke, 9.25 to 1 compression ratio. Four-barrel carburetor, 5-bearing crankshaft, chain-drive timing, hydraulic valve lifters, heavy-duty oil-bath air cleaner, dual exhaust system.		
Corvette V8	Valve-in-head V8 engine. 225 h.p. at 5200 rpm; torque, 270 ft-lbs at 3600 rpm. 265 cubic inch displacement. 3.75" bore, 3.0" stroke, 9.25 to 1 compression ratio. Dual four-barrel carburetors, two oil-bath air cleaners, special high-lift camshaft, high-speed mechanical valve lifters, high-power exhaust headers, dual exhaust system.		
Clutch	Diaphragm spring type with permanently lubricated throw-out bearing. 9½" diameter on Six; 10" diameter on Turbo-Fire V8. Coil spring type, 10" diameter on Super Turbo-Fire V8 and Corvette V8.		None
Transmission	Heavy-Duty Transmission 3-speed, synchro-mesh selective gear transmission, with gearshift lever on steering column. Gear Ratios: First . . . . 2.94 to 1 Second . . . . 1.68 to 1 Third . . . . 1.00 to 1 Reverse . . . . 2.94 to 1	Heavy-Duty Transmission plus Overdrive* 3-pinion, planetary gear overdrive, providing automatic fourth speed; gear ratio, 0.71 to 1. Accelerator control: Electric cut-in, through releasing treadle, above 30 mph.; down-shift to direct drive by pressing treadle to floor. Pull-out knob locks out overdrive.	Automatic Transmission* Hydraulic, 3-element torque converter, with planetary gears for reverse and low. Selector lever on steering column. Safety switch in starter circuit. Oil cooler integrated with engine cooling system. Maximum torque converter ratio, 2.1 to 1. Planetary gear ratio, 1.82 to 1. Maximum overall ratio, 3.82 to 1.
Rear Axle	Semi-floating, with hypoid gears. Single-unit "banjo" housing. Hotchkiss drive.		
	3.70 to 1 ratio	4.11 to 1 ratio	3.55 to 1 ratio

*Optional at extra cost.

1956

1956 Bel Air Sport Coupe

1956 Two-Ten 2-door Sedan

An interesting variant initially appeared in 1956. The Del Rey Club Coupe (below), based on the above Two-Ten 2-door Sedan had the roominess of the sedan, but featured a washable, all vinyl interior including side walls and headliner (lower photo).

Mr. Jeff Frank, Laguna Beach, California

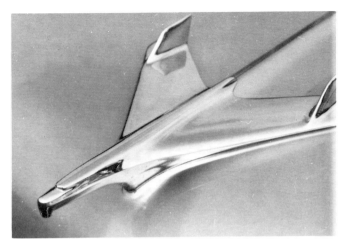

The new wider grill sharply changes the appearance of the front end (page 185) broadening the appearance of the car.

Although generally similar to the 1955 hood ornament, the 1956 version has a longer "tail".

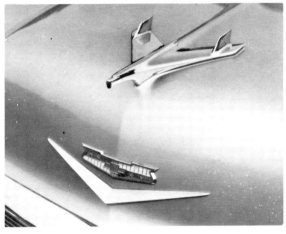

The grill is extended to the sides of the car, wrapping neatly around the parking lights.

An emphatic new V-shaped ornament is added beneath the hood emblem on cars equipped with the V-8 engine.

The hood emblem again changes, becoming narrower than the 1955 style.

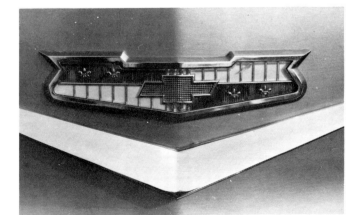

A series of horizontal bright metal bars in the new grill add apparent width to the car.

New rectangular parking lights replace the tear-drop shaped lamps of 1955.

The bumper continues to be wrapped protectively around the corner of the fenders.

The front fenders have a new, flatter, visor extending over the headlamps necessitating a new lamp bezel (compare page 187).

Wheel size remains at 15 inches, tires are 6.70 x 15. Full wheel covers are supplied with the Bel Air models only and are extra-cost options on the others.

The Two-Ten Series has its own distinctive single-stripe side trim. Its emphasizing fin just above the front wheel is omitted on the One-Fifty models.

Inside rear view mirrors are supported from the windshield header.

All models now have decorative bright metal windshield frame trim, but that on the One-Fifty Series is narrower.

Dual windshield wipers are standard on all models as is the ventilation intake at the base of the windshield.

An outside rear view mirror is an accessory, not standard equipment.

The wrap-around windshield introduced in 1955 is unchanged.

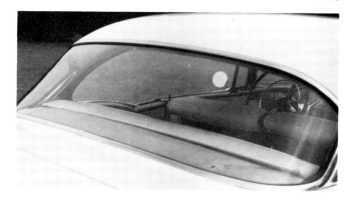

The narrow center "posts" of the Sport Coupe and the new 4-door Sport Sedan will lower with the windows to provide unobstructed vision.

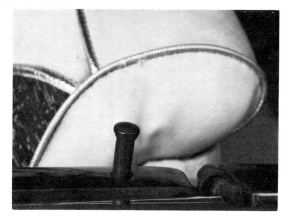

Inside door locks are provided on all models.

Bright metal trim around the windows is a feature only of the Bel Air Models and Two-Ten Sport Models.

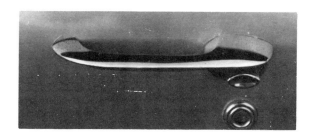

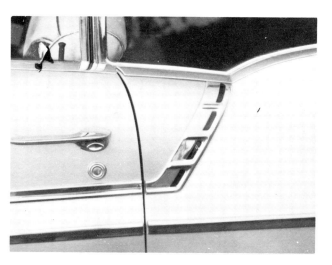

A simulated "air scoop" moulding is used on the sides.

1956

The Bel Air models have a dual-stripe on their sides which provides an effective two-tone possibility.

The Two-Ten models have a characteristic single stripe broken by the simulated air scoop.

A Chevrolet script nameplate appears on the rear fenders of the Two-Ten and One-Fifty models.

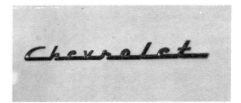

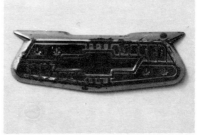

The Bel Air script and the emblem are separate pieces and are placed so that the emblem is *behind* the script on both rear fenders (above) and (below).

The rear wheel housing is now tear-drop shaped (compare page 190) and add a sense of forward motion to the appearance. The gas tank flap has been eliminated from the fender (next page).

The V-shaped emphasis trim beneath the new rear ornament is only used on cars equipped with one of the V-8 engine options.

New tail lights include a place for back-up lights, but these remain extra cost options

The gas tank filler cap is now located beneath the left rear tail light. To reach it, a latch at its top is rotated slightly (right) and the lamp housing rotates (below).

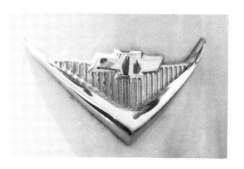

These decorative emblems are used only on V-8 engined cars.

A new rear deck lid emblem mathes the one on the hood. The V-shaped trim below it indicates a V-8 engine.

A large luggage compartment is provided. A rubber mat is installed on its floor, but its side walls are not trimmed. Jacking instructions are placed behind the spare tire. The lid has a locating pin and latch (top photo) which engage appropriate fixtures on the sill (left).

The vent windows (called "ventipanes" in the Chevrolet literature) are provided with inside locks.

The interior of the Bel Air Sport Coupe and Sport Sedan is upholstered in a pattern cloth with Ivory leather-grain vinyl trim. The headliner in these models and the Nomad is vinyl, in the other models, cloth.

Rotary locks are used on all doors.

The "dog-leg" resulting from the vertical windshield pillar is mildly obtrusive and limits access. As much for this reason as any other, it was later eliminated.

The instrument panel is continued in the 1955 style, and continues to feature the two matching instrument housings.

A clear view of the speedometer and instruments is obtained through the steering wheel.

The unique three-spoke Bel Air wheel is continued; other models have a two-spoke steering wheel. All are 18" diameter, but only the Bel Air and the Two-Ten models have a full-circle horn ring.

The distinctive Bel Air steering wheel continues to feature a special emblem at its hub.

The speedometer cluster is fundamentally unchanged from the 1955 style. The shift indicator continues to be housed at its base when Powerglide is installed. Direction signals are standard on all models for the first time.

The distinctive "bow-tie" instrument panel trim of 1955 (page 198) was replaced in 1956 with a less involved pattern.

The ignition switch continues to offer a non-locked OFF position in which the key may be withdrawn.

Three optional radios are offered again in 1956. This is the new Wonderbar, a signal seeking push button version, the most expensive.

This is the Push Button radio. Less expensive than the Wonderbar, it is yet more costly than the Manual Tuning version which was also available. 1956 was the first year in which the two Civil Defense tuning locations were marked by appropriate dots on the dial (above).

If no radio was ordered, a blanking panel which matches the rest of the instrument panel trim was supplied.

The cigarette lighter is standard on the Bel Air and the Two-Ten Series, and "extra" on the One-Fifty Models.

The Bell Air script appears only on the models of that Series, (Two-Ten and One-Fifty cars have a Chevrolet script on their radio grill). The electric clock is standard on the Bel Air series only.

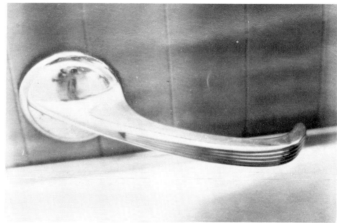

Bel Air and Two-Ten Series door hardware.

1956 NOMAD

1956 Bel Air Nomad   *Mr. Brad Dunn, Chula Vista, California*

1956 Bel Air Nomad

The top-of-the-line Chevrolet model, the Nomad 6-passenger, 2-door luxury-trimmed station wagon, was continued in 1956. Again distinctive in its own right, it shared a unique 1956 appearance emphasized by the Bel Air dual stripe on its side.

Mr. Carl Pikus, Vista, California

1956 NOMAD

The 1956 Nomad shares the frontal appearance of the rest of the Bel Air line to which it belongs. It dose not have extra trim such as the stripes placed over the headlights of the 1955 Nomad (page 206).

Unmistakably trim, the rear quarter view of a Nomad shows a model unlike any other.

A distinctive Nomad sloped pillar remains unchanged. The simulated air scoop trim at its base is not interchangeable with that on other models.

Bel Air Series' dual stripe lends itself admirably to two-tone paint selections.

Nomad is provided with wide doors for best access to the rear seat.

The pattern of embossed ribs continues on the Nomad roof.

As on all models of the Bel Air Series, the trailing edge of the side trim emphasizes the new shape of the rear fender wheel well openings.

The wrap-around rear quarter window continues. Only the forward section can be opened for ventilation.

From the rear a different tail light quickly identifies this as a 1956, not 1955, Nomad.

With tailgate lowered and lift gate open, a wide loading hatch is presented.

The lift gate is supported by a latching telescope hinge (left).

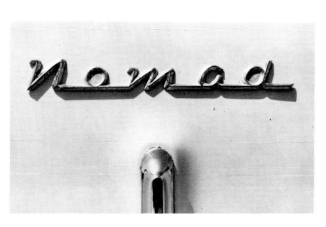

Nomad script is unchanged.

The tailgate is supported in its loading position by two flexible steel cables.

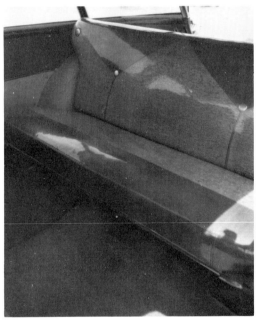

The spare tire and jack is stored beneath a hinged panel at the rear of the station wagons.

The second seat can be folded into the floor for added cargo space. A rod-like auxiliary "leg" provides added support for the rotated seat cushion.

The tailgate, the rear floor, the back of the rear seat, and the underside of the rear seat cushion platform are covered with a sturdy ribbed rubber-like material.

Two dome lights are provided in the Nomad, one just above each quarter pillar.

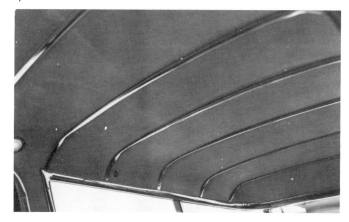

The attractive decorative chromed "bows" are continued in the Nomad.

CHEVROLET 1957

You'll feel a very special kind of pride the day you park a new Chevrolet in your driveway. Maybe you'll even find yourself looking out the window, now and then, just for the pleasure of seeing it there. It's a beautiful sight to behold—fresh and alert, with a certain ready-to-go spirit written all over it.

And when the neighbors drop by to "look 'er over," they'll be prouder than ever. They'll see fine construction and finishing touches everywhere. They'll feel the extra solidity of Body by Fisher, and they'll see the deeper luster of Chevy's lacquer paint job.

Then they'll want a ride around the block to see if Chevrolet is as sweet, smooth and sassy as it looks. That's how people become happy Chevy owners. Stop by your Chevrolet dealer's and you'll see what we mean. . . . Chevrolet Division of General Motors, Detroit 2, Mich.

More people drive Chevrolets than any other car.

You get more
to be proud of in a Chevy!

BEL AIR SERIES
  2-door Sedan
  4-door Sedan
  Sport Sedan   (4-door hardtop)
  Sport Coupe   (2-door hardtop)
  Convertible
  Nomad   (2-door 6-passenger station wagon)
  Townsman   (4-door 6-passenger station wagon)

TWO-TEN SERIES
  2-door Sedan
  4-door Sedan
  Sport Sedan   (4-door hardtop)
  Sport Coupe   (2-door hardtop)
  Delray Club Coupe
  Beauville   (4-door 9-passenger station wagon)
  Townsman   (4-door 6-passenger station wagon)
  Handyman   (2-door 6-passenger station wagon)

ONE-FIFTY SERIES
  2-door Sedan
  4-door Sedan
  Utility Sedan
  Handyman   (2-door 6-passenger station wagon)

1957 brought several changes, including Chevrolet's first offer of optional Fuel Injection and an all-new automatic transmission, Turboglide, which was offered along with the earlier Powerglide. Corvette was now included with the passenger car illustrations (although it also rated its own sales literature), and Chevrolet made its first use of the word "hardtop" in describing its attractive Sport models.

In the massive Super Turbo-Fire 283, Chevrolet's new fuel injection option boosted rated horsepower to 283, but for the first time, Chevrolet preferred to delete that characteristic and referred only to cubic inch displacement. This was regrettable because for the first time ever in a domestic engine Chevrolet had achieved an output of one horsepower per cubic inch displacement.

All cars were built on the 115" chassis, and models and Series designations remained about the same (although the 1956 Bel Air "Beauville" became the 1957 Bel Air "Townsman"), but despite an unwillingness to advertise horsepower as an engine characteristic, Chevrolet's 1957 engine and transmission selection choice was unbelievable. In addition to the former Blue Flame Six, there were both a 265 cid and a 283 cid "Turbo-Fire" V-8 and the new 283 cubic inch "Super Turbo-Fire 283" engine offered in both a 4-barrel carburetor standard version and also with twin 4-barrel carburetors as the "Corvette V-8" option. Beyond that, a maximum performance version with fuel injection, two exhausts, special valve system, mechanical lifters, and other features, brought the V-8 version options to a total of five choices.

Full power options were continued including Power Steering, Brakes, Seats, and Windows, as well as Air Conditioning, and optional Overdrive and Powerglide transmissions were joined by the new Turboglide which incorporates three turbines to provide an infinitely variable torque ratio for smoothest acceleration from start to full speed.

The 1957 styling has to be among the best ever done by Chevrolet, and marks a high point in the appearance of cars of this era. The following year a new longer chassis and consequent body redesign created a whole new appearance.

...THE POWER TEAM OF YOUR CHOICE

All power teams available in all **Bel Air**, **"Two-Ten"** and **"One-Fifty"** models. See your Chevrolet dealer for the price of the power team you prefer.	Turboglide	Powerglide	Overdrive	Synchro-Mesh*
"Corvette V8" 283-cu.-in. V8, 9.5:1 c.r. Twin 4-barrel carburetion**	●	●	●	●
"Super Turbo-Fire 283" 283-cu.-in. V8, 9.5:1 c.r. Single 4-barrel carburetion	●	●	●	●
"Turbo-Fire 283" 283-cu.-in. V8, 8.5:1 c.r. 2-barrel carburetion	●	●		
"Turbo-Fire 265" 265-cu.-in. V8, 8.0:1 c.r. 2-barrel carburetion			●	●
"Blue-Flame" 235-cu.-in. Six, 8.0:1 c.r. Single-barrel carburetion		●	●	●

*Choice of regular Synchro-Mesh or special close-ratio 3-speed available with "Corvette V8" engine only.

**Fuel injection system also available with all transmissions except Overdrive.

All Chevrolet engines feature highly efficient valve-in-head design, aluminum pistons, automatic choke, positive-shift starter, forged steel crankshaft, 12-volt electrical system, full pressure lubrication. Full dual exhaust system standard on "Corvette V8" and "Super Turbo-Fire 283." Hydraulic valve lifters on all power teams shown above. Maximum performance version of "Corvette V8" available with close-ratio Synchro-Mesh on special order features fuel injection system, 9.5 to 1 compression ratio, competition-type camshaft, and high-speed valve system with special valve springs, spring dampers, and mechanical valve lifters.

LUXURY—IN AND OUT

All 1957 Chevrolet models are available in a wide range of exterior colors in either solid tone or two-tone combinations, with distinctive two-tone interiors keyed to exterior color. Your Chevrolet dealer can show you all these exciting exterior colors and actual samples of every fine fabric and costly vinyl interior material.

Bel Air Series—the ultimate in luxury, with gold anodized aluminum grille screen and decorative accents. Ribbed two-tone silver anodized aluminum panel on rear fender and bright metal body sill molding are optional at extra cost. Seven two-tone interiors keyed to exterior color.

"Two-Ten" and **"One-Fifty"** Series feature silver anodized aluminum grille screen and bright metal decorative accents. Three two-tone interiors, keyed to exterior color. "One-Fifty" sedan interior harmonizes with exterior color. Handyman offers two two-tone interiors, keyed to exterior color.

EXTRA SAFETY ALL AROUND

Rugged all-steel body structure with unitized side panels, double-walled doors, triple-safe door latches, welded-in instrument panel, and central roof bow on all closed models. High quality polished lacquer finish. Convenient single key lock system. High volume ventilation system with air inlets above headlights. Counterbalanced hood with positive safety latch. Concealed deck lid hinges. Hydraulic-powered top on convertible.

FIRM FOUNDATION

Extra-rigid welded box girder frame (special center X in convertible). Glide-Ride front suspension with independent coil springs, low-friction spherical joints, and exclusive anti-dive braking action. Outrigger rear suspension, with extra-long permanently lubricated leaf springs. Life-sealed double-acting shock absorbers. Luxury-cushion 7.50-14 4-ply (6-ply on 9-passenger station wagon) tubeless tires. Powerful hydraulic self-energizing Jumbo-Drum brakes with 11" drums and bonded linings. Mechanical parking brake on both rear wheels. Exclusive Ball-Race steering gear with balanced linkage. Proved 12-volt electrical system, 54-plate battery with 36-month warranty. Precision-aimed sealed beam headlights. Built-in directional signals. Rear axle ratio matched to power team: Synchro-Mesh, 3.55:1; Overdrive, 4.11:1; Powerglide and Turboglide, 3.36:1. Fuel tank capacity: station wagons, 17 gallons; other models, 16 gallons.

MEASURES OF QUALITY

Wheelbase, 115". Front tread 58.0", rear tread, 58.8". Overall dimensions: length 202.8"; width 73.9"; loaded height 60.5" (sport coupe, sport sedan, convertible 59.1", station wagons 60.8").

THESE ARE OPTIONAL AT EXTRA COST

Power steering. Power brakes. Power windows. Power front seat. E-Z-Eye glass. Padded instrument panel. Heater. Air Conditioner. Electric windshield wipers. White sidewall tires (rayon or nylon cord). Heavy-duty 6-ply tires. Heavy-duty clutch, heavy-duty rear springs, and other mechanical features. Safety belt, shoulder harness, choice of radios, and full range of other accessory equipment.

1957 Bel Air Sport Coupe

Mr. Bob Wingate, San Dimas, Californ.

This car is equipped with optional fuel injection.

1957 Two-Ten 4-door Sedan

1957 One-Fifty 4-door Sedan

1957

A new styling feature joins the grill with the bumper in one flowing design.

The hood now has two "windsplits" running its length.

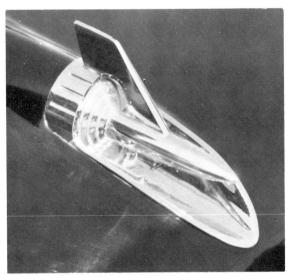

A new chromed spear decoration is used at the forward end of each of the two hood windsplits (upper right).

In place of the former emblem, a script nameplate now appears on the hood. The V-shaped emblem denoting "V-8 engine" is gold in color on the Bel Air Series, chromed on the Two-Ten and One-Fifty cars that have the V-8.

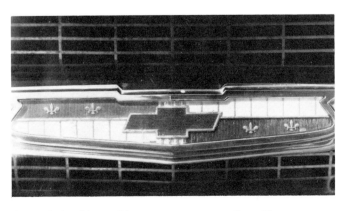

A restyled, wider emblem now appears on the grill.

The parking lights are placed at the ends of the center grill bar.

The parking light housings are visored for extra effect. Behind them, the grill of the Bel Air Series only is anodized in gold; others are chromed.

The three "stripes" on the front fenders suggest air intakes, but are actually decorative only. On the Bel Air Series, only, (above) gold inserts are used to emphasize the stripe.

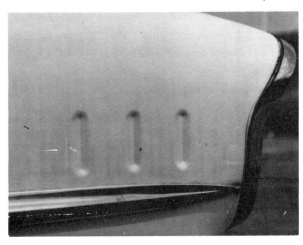

A full-width wrap-around front bumper adds to the massive appearance of the front end.

The headlights of all models are provided with chromed fender trim simulating air intakes around the lamps.

The standard treatment is a decorative blanking plate simulating a lamp (right). Options include driving lights, and a rubber bumper (above) as dress-up items.

The wheel diameter has been decreased by one inch to lower the car and tires are now 7.50 x 14. Blackwalls are standard, whitewalls a popular option.

The windshield on all models has a decorative bright metal frame.

The standard mirror (above) is often replaced with a non-glare accessory (left).

The vent air intake grill at the base of the windshield (page 220) has been eliminated.

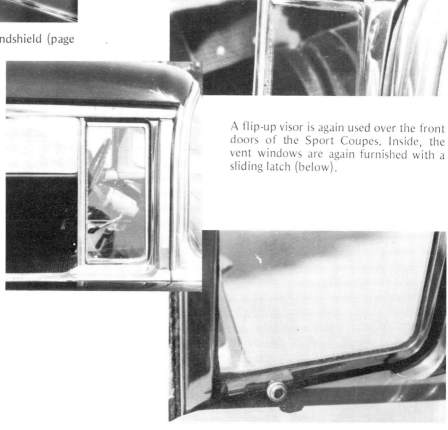

A flip-up visor is again used over the front doors of the Sport Coupes. Inside, the vent windows are again furnished with a sliding latch (below).

The radio antenna is mounted on the right front fender.

The rear quarter pillar of the Sport Coupes and the Bel Air 4-door Sedan are trimmed with bright metal mouldings which are not found on the other models.

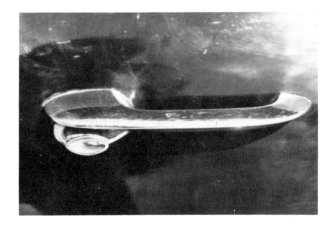

The car above is a Two-Ten Series 4-door Sedan. The lower stripe is conventional trim; the upper stripe and the Chevrolet nameplate above it (upper photo) were early-season additions and do not appear in early catalogs. The Bel Air Series (upper right) features a gold emblem and series nameplate (right).

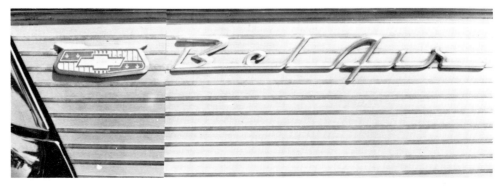

This is a factory option outside rear view mirror. Note the distinctive "bow-tie" insignia on its back.

Outside rear view mirrors are accessory equipment, and are not furnished as standard items.

The attractive ribbed two-tone silver anodized aluminum panel on the rear fender, and the metal body sill moulding below it are exclusive Bel Air options.

The sharply pointed, high trailing edges of the 1957 fenders are unusually distinctive.

Rear deck ornaments, V-8 engine models

Rear deck ornament, six-cylinder models

A hinged door in the left rear fender opens to expose the fuel filler tube.

The rear license plate light is built into the bumper below it.

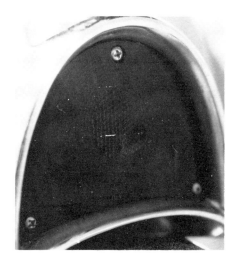

The Stop and Tail Light functions are built into a housing (upper right) at the base of the fender. Balancing it, beneath the bumper, is a simulated exhaust outlet. Between them is a decorative plate which is removed when optional back-up lights (above) are installed.

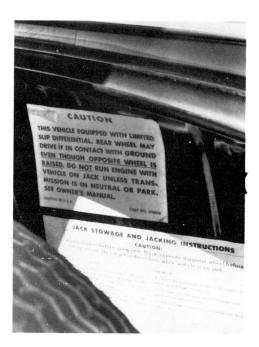

Installation of optional Positraction, a limited slip differential, is noted on a warning sticker placed above the jacking instructions.

The floor of the luggage compartment is level and packages need not be lifted over obstructions to gain access.

A ribbed rubber floor mat protects the luggage compartment.

Inside door locks are furnished on all models.

The Serial Number plate continues to appear on the left front door pillar.

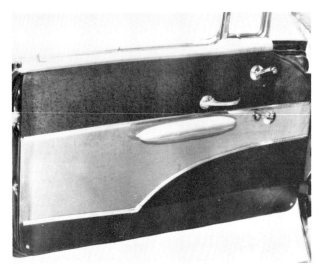

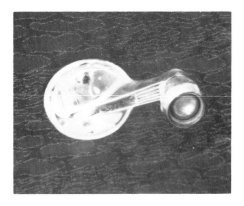

Two-tone interiors are featured in all models, but those of the Bel Air Series are more elaborate than others.

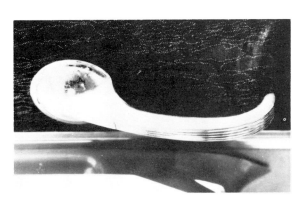

The 1957 Instrument Panel has been completely redesigned, and in addition to a re-grouping, it features a visored instrument cluster.

The horn button of the One-Fifty Series has only an emblem.

The Bel Air Series has a two-spoke steering wheel with a full circle horn ring. At its hub, the series name appears along with a small emblem.

A full-circle horn ring is also used on the Two-Ten cars and the series name appears on the hub button.

A round speedometer returns, replacing the unusual pie-shaped 1956 model (page 227).

The segment at the base of the speedometer is used to display the optional automatic transmission gear position. This is the familiar Powerglide (P-N-D-L-R) pattern which is replaced in Turboglide with a more conventional P-R-N-D-(L) pattern.

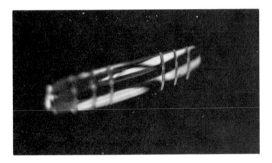

The T-shaped parking brake handle is continued.

Above the gasoline gauge are two lamps to indicate Right Turn (direction signal) and failure of the generator to charge.

Above the Temperature gauge are lamps to indicate Left Turn and Low Oil Pressure.

A new distinctive trim pattern appears on the instrument panel.

A standard removable blanking plate conceals the radio mounting.

The Wonder Bar radio is one of three options again this year.

This is the low-priced manual tuning optional radio. Also available is a pushbutton model.

The electric clock is standard in the Bel Air models. A blanking plate (below right) is furnished in the others, along with the script nameplate (above left) substituted for Bel Air (above).

The controls for the economy Heater (above) or the higher-priced Ventilating Heater & Defroster which mixes outside air (right) fit into the instrument panel. A third option, Air Conditioning, has an interchangeable control head (page 260).

By the mid-Fifties, Chevrolet had correctly determined the interest of a large number of post-war families with young children in appropriate vehicles for their special purpose. Large enough to seat them all, the automobile had also to double as a utility vehicle. In particular, women seemed to want the convenience of a ruggedly upholstered car into which bulky (and sometimes leaking) grocery packages could easily be placed.

Thus, by 1957, Chevrolet's station wagon choices included a total of six models ranging from the luxury-appointed two-door Nomad (page 264) to an economy Handyman in the One-Fifty Series which slightly resembled it, and all featured fold-down rear seats to increase cargo space.

1957 Bel Air Townsman

Mr. Steve Beechler, San Marcos, California

The windows are self-framed in the doors, and the wide pillars behind the doors are therefore quite obvious.

The windows in the doors can be lowered, but the rear quarter glass is fixed.

Two doors on each side, hinged at their front edge, provide easy access to the interior.

The rear quarter pillar is painted, not bright-metal trimmed.

A locking handle is turned to release the tail gate latch.

The sharply-pointed rear fenders extend well past the body.

The Chevrolet script is standard; the emblem beneath it, as always, indicates the installation of one of the V-8 engine options.

The tailgate is unadorned by additional trim stripes as on the Nomad (page 268).

The headliners in the station wagons are sewn, but have concealed bows.

The uniquely patterned original upholstery is protected by accessory clear vinyl seatcovers installed by a later owner.

With the rear seat folded, an unobstructed cargo space of over 80 cubic feet is provided.

An accessory external sun visor is designed attractively to follow the existing contours.

Under the visor can be seen a prism, another accessory, (below). This ingenious device permits a driver better to see an overhead traffic signal.

A non-glare inside rear view mirror, panel-mounted, replaces the standard unit (page 245).

A decal is placed on the vent window.

This control head interchanges with the others (page 213).

Air Conditioning first offered in the 1955 models, remained an accessory of somewhat limited purchase. When installed, however, the system was well integrated and had none of the appearance of an after-market installation.

Vents are built into the instrument panel.

The compressor is belt-driven and placed on the right side of the engine.

An auxiliary radiator and condenser are installed ahead of the engine coolant radiator.

An accessory Continental Spare Tire kit extends car length.

An accessory brake warning light appears under the instrument panel.

Optional Power Brakes have a special foot pedal.

Unlike the 1956 kits (above), the *1957* accessory features a solid rear faceplate.

A concealed release mechanism permits the spare wheel to be moved for access to the trunk.

Accessory trim at the base of the rear deck lid matches the special Bel Air accessory side trim.

1957 FUEL INJECTION

A script nameplate and the crossed flag insignia is placed on the front fenders (photo left).

Already well-filled, the engine compartment barely accepts the accessory.

A now highly sought after passenger car "accessory" introduced in 1957 is "Fuel Injection". Actually, the term refers to the special "Super Turbo-Fire 283" Corvette engine on one version of which this system was factory-installed. In addition to fuel injection, the engine had a 10.5:1 compression ratio (against 8.0:1 for the "standard" V-8), competition-type camshaft, and a special high-speed valve system featuring among other important performance items, special valve springs, dampers, and mechanical valve lifters.

With its displacements of 283 cubic inches, this mighty engine was rated at 283 horsepower (at 6200 rpm) in this maximum-performance configuration, achieving the highly unique rated output of <u>one horsepower per cubic inch displacement.</u>

A special air cleaner filters and ducts incoming air.

The control device to the left of the special fuel injection manifold senses fuel requirements and adjusts a butterfly valve in the metering assembly at the right center.

Fuel injection is simply a constant flow fuel system which delivers the fuel directly to the cylinders thus eliminating the customary carburetor. This device was offered in 1957 on the maximum-performance version of Chevrolet's new 283 cubic inch V-8 engine. Another option offered dual 4-barrel carburetors for a slightly less 270 horsepower rating.

Another version of the new Super Turbo-Fire 283 delivers 185 horsepower equipped with a 2-barrel carburetor. The hose return to the air cleaner is a California-required crankcase ventilator.

1957 NOMAD

1957 Bel Air Nomad

The attractive 2-door Bel Air 6-passenger Nomad station wagon continues for 1957 with the expected trim changes shown here. Of limited contemporary interest, only about 6100 were produced, and the new Bel Air Townsman, a 4-door station wagon outsold it by a factor of almost five to one.

Nathaniel Watterson, Jr. Spring Valley, California

1957 NOMAD

The 1957 Bel Air side trim appears on the Nomad as it does on others in the Series.

The slanted side pillar, a distinctive characteristic of the Nomad, is continued.

Only the forward portion of the quarter window may be opened for ventilation.

Bright metal trim frames the glass in the quarter windows and lift gate.

The stripe atop the rear fenders (above and at the left) appears on all Series. Shorter on the Two Ten and One Fifty, it extends forward almost three feet on the Bel Air models.

The rear fenders extend substantially beyond the back of the body.

A license plate light is built into the rear fender guards.

1957 NOMAD

The nameplate again appears on the tail gate, but this script differs slightly from the earlier version (page 235). Again, the V-shaped emblem indicates a V-8 engine installation.

Seven trim stripes, six of which are visible here, are continued on the Nomad tail gate.

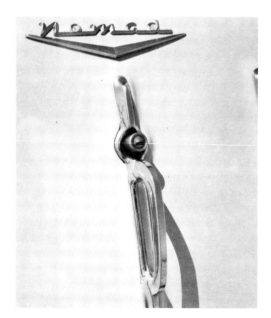

The locking tail gate latch release button is unchanged.

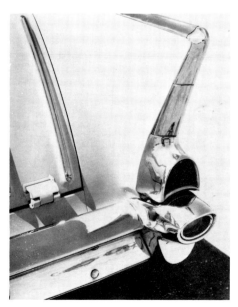

External hinges support the tail gate at either end.

Never a successful seller, the beautiful Chevrolet Nomad had only reached a <u>total</u> production of just over 22,000 in its three model-years, and 40% of that was the first year, 1955, before its novelty wore off.

Generally not one to persist when the economics suggested change, Chevrolet elected to eliminate the luxury two-door station wagon with the production of the last 1957 Nomad. The portion of the Market that had been attracted to the name was favored with its continuation on the luxury leader of Chevrolet's 1958 station wagon line, a 4-door six passenger station wagon.

IT GOES BIG . . . WITH SPECTACULAR NEW SHAPE!

CHEVROLET
1958

BEL AIR SERIES
Impala Sport Coupe
Impala Convertible
2-door Sedan
4-door Sedan
Sport Coupe (2-door hardtop)
Sport Sedan (4-door hardtop)

BISCAYNE SERIES
2-door Sedan
4-door Sedan

DELRAY Series
2-door Coupe (2-door Sedan)
Utility Sedan (2-door, 3-passenger Sedan)
4-door Sedan

STATION WAGON SERIES
Nomad
(4-door, 6-passenger)   (4-d
Brookwood
(4-door, 9- passenger)
Brookwood
(4-door, 6-passenger)
Yeoman
(4-door, 6-passenger)
Yeoman
(2-door, 6-passenger)

New! All New!

1958 brought a totally new Chevrolet. Built on a new 117.5 inch wheelbase Safety-Girder chassis the all-new bodies were 9 inches longer than the 1957 models and presented a substantially revised appearance. Optional air suspension was offered for smoother ride, but even without it, the new four-wheel coil suspension gave a softer, more cushioned ride.

The sturdy Blue Flame Six, now rated at 145 horsepower, (achieved with slightly higher compression ratio), was continued, but the old 265 cubic inch Turbo-Fire V-8 was discontinued in favor of the Super Turbo-Fire 283 introduced last year. This was offered in versions with 2-barrel, 4-barrel, and Fuel Injection which brought its rating to 290 horsepower. New for the year was the big-bore Turbo-Thrust V-8 engine, a 348 cubic inch displacement giant which in its maximum-performance mechanical valve lifter version equipped with three 2-barrel carburetors developed a whopping 315 horsepower at 5600 rpm.

In addition to the standard three-speed synchro-mesh transmission, options again included Overdrive, Powerglide, and the three-turbine Turboglide.

The Series names were beginning to fade. Although Impala was introduced this year as a sub-series of the Bel Air Series, it was soon to supplant that name. The former Two-Ten Series had become the Biscayne Series, now reduced to only two models, and the old One-Fifty Series was now the Delray, and included 3 models.

Noting increased interest in the body style, the station wagon models were grouped as a separate Series that provided everything from the luxury 4-door 6-passenger Nomad (replacing the earlier 2-door model of the same name) through an economy 2-door 6-passenger Yeoman in five model choices.

Chevrolet Nomad—4-door 6-passenger

NEW WAGONS WITH WONDERFUL WAYS— THESE NEW '58 CHEVROLETS!

There's new lilt in their looks, new verve in their ways. And you have five to choose from. Pick a two-door model or four, six-passenger or nine, you'll more in the smartest station wagon set there is!

You never had handsomer reasons to move into a new wagon. These 1958 Chevrolets are trim, low, wide—nine crisp inches longer!

Notice that the larger liftgate curves clear around at the corners. It's hinged into the roof and raises completely out of the way for easier loading and maximum-size loads.

Chevrolet's new standard Full Coil suspension puts an extra-soft cushioning of deep coil springs at every wheel. Or, you can have the ultimate of a real air ride—Level Air suspension.* Bumps get swallowed up in cushions of air. And your wagon automatically keeps its normal level, regardless of how heavy the load.

There's a livelier thrifty Blue-Flame 6. And a potent new 250-h.p. Turbo-Thrust V8,* an ideal mate for honey-smooth Turboglide* drive. See your Chevrolet dealer. . . . Chevrolet Division of General Motors, Detroit 2, Michigan.

*Optional at extra cost.

CHEVROLET

Chevrolet Brookwood—4-door 6-passenger

The attractive Bel Air Sport Sedan, a four-door hardtop model introduced in 1956, continues to be a popular model.

Photo courtesy Chevrolet Motor Division

1958

Quite similar to the better-known Impala Sport Coupe, this Bel Air Sport Coupe was also offered in 1958. Substantially the same model, it differed principally in external trim, and was shortly replaced by the Impala model.

1958 Bel Air Impala Sport Coupe

Photo courtesy of Chevrolet Motor Division

The 1958 Delray Utility Sedan continued Chevrolet's practice of offering a three-passenger sedan with added storage space behind its single seat. It was essentially the 2-door Sedan (which appears in their literature as a "Coupe") with its rear seat omitted.

Fairway Chevrolet, Las Vegas, Nevada

With a new wide grill dual headlights, and a massive wrap-around bumper, the appearance of a much larger car emerges.

The 1958 model is the first Chevrolet to employ dual headlamps. The lamps are somewhat smaller in diameter than the earlier style.

On the Bel Air Series only, a bright metal trim stripe is affixed to the top of the front fenders.

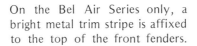

The Biscayne and Delray models do not have the trim stripe on their fenders.

Matching the dual headlamps, new dual parking lights are placed in the grill.

An emblem returns to the hood replacing the script used in 1957.

The new grill eliminates the former heavy bars and substitutes an interesting new pattern.

This elaborately striped side trim is used on the Bel Air Series only.

The front fenders of all models are embossed with four distinctive stripes. On the Bel Air Series only, bright metal inserts dress up the appearance.

A new rear view mirror appears.

A ventilating air intake grill returns to the cowl at the base of the windshield.

The windshield pillars slant abruptly backwards resulting in a new shape for the vent windows.

The outside door handles with the distinctive oval push button, first seen in 1955 are continued.

The outside rear view mirror remains an accessory.

The distinctively heavy Bel Air Series trim stripe continues down the side of the car.

The Impala was a new sub-series of the Bel Air line and initially included only a Sport Coupe and the Convertible. Differing in trim, these models had a new emblem on the quarter.

This bright metal simulated air exhaust was used on the Impala models only.

The rear wheel housings continue in the tear-shaped style first seen in 1956. No rear wheel cover panels were offered.

Matching the four bright metal trim stripes on the front fenders of the Impala are these distinctive Bel Air Series stripes on the rear fenders.

This panel above the rear bumper is hinged and opens (above right) to provide access to the fuel filler cap.

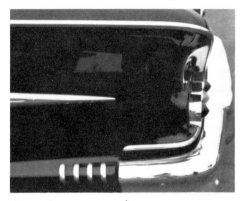

A massive new rear bumper sweeps protectively around the fenders.

Only the Impala Sport Coupe has this simulated air exhaust vent above its rear window.

From the rear, the 1958 fenders have a distinctive and unique look.

Although an emblem is again used on the hood, the Chevrolet script is continued on the rear deck lid. Decorative V-shaped trim is used on V-8 equipped cars.

Three lamps are placed on each rear fender. The center one is a back-up light, the outer one is the standard directional signal light, and the inner lamps are marker lights.

A new rear deck lid latch appears.

A larger luggage compartment now appears. Its floor is covered with a protective rubber mat, and the spare tire is stored vertically on the right side.

Both a front fender or a rear-mounted radio antenna were available in 1958.

The rear deck lid is relatively flat, adding to the longer appearance of the new body style.

An entirely new look is provided by a visored instrument panel which now sweeps around smoothly onto the doors.

The new deep-hub steering wheel is restyled and provides a new slim appearance.

At the hub of the Impala steering wheel appears a crossed-flag insignia which is not used on the other models.

New for 1958 is a foot-operated parking brake which is provided with a manual release lever just under the instrument panel.

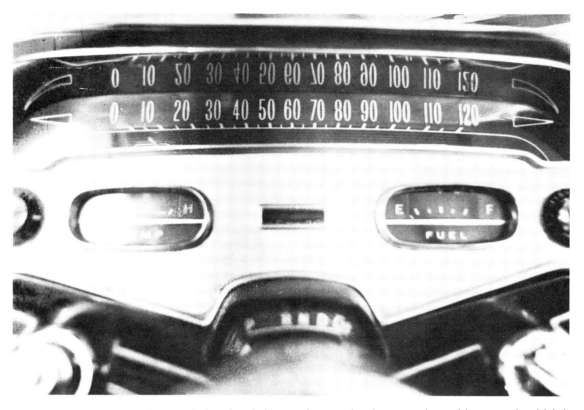

The instrument panel has been redesigned and the speedometer has become a long, thin rectangle which is installed with a reflective bright metal trim above it. The standard direction signal indicators appear at the ends of the speedometer housing.

Only Temperature (left) and Fuel (right) gauges are provided. Lights, placed behind appropriately lettered rectangular "windows" just beneath the ends of the speedometer scale illuminate to indicate low oil pressure or a non-functioning electrical system.

Again a transmission gear position indicator appears on the instrument panel at the base of the steering column. Powerglide and also Turboglide are again offered as options.

Manual, Push Button, and Wonderbar (above) radio options were again offered for 1958 and each was available with either a front or rear-fender-mounted external antenna.

The non-locking ignition switch continues in use.

Controls for the heater are built into the lower part of the instrument panel.

A concealed ash tray is provided.

1958

An electric clock is standard in the luxury Impala.

An accessory, a rear seat radio speaker is concealed behind the standard grill (above) and controlled by a knob on the instrument panel (right).

1958 Biscayne 4-door Sedan

Photo courtesy Chevrolet Motor Division

The new bodies have a wider door pillar, and for convenience the Serial Number Plate is now installed in a horizontal position. The courtesy light switches in the front doors are omitted on the Delray Series and the Yeoman station wagons.

New inside door hardware is introduced featuring smaller diameter hubs and with large escutcheon plates added for appearance. The knobs on the window cranks are of a new design.

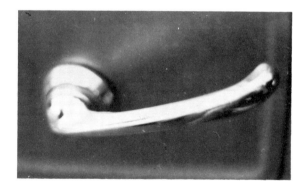

A bright metal trim cap is used at the forward end of the arm rests whose rear portion is styled to include a safety reflector visible from the rear when the door is opened.

1958 Bel Air Impala Convertible with accessory Continental kit.

The attractive Bel Air Impala Convertible features a fully automatic folding top. After releasing latches above the windshield, the rest of the sequence is automatically controlled by operating a knob under the instrument panel.

This is an accessory Continental kit which removes the spare tire from the Luggage compartment and at the same time adds to the external appearance.

1958 Brookwood 4-door 9-passenger station wagon

Photo courtesy of Chevrolet Motor Division

Beginning in 1958, the 2-door Nomad luxury-trimmed station wagon was replaced by a 4-door model which continued to bear the former name.

1958 Bel Air Nomad 4-door 6-passenger station wagon

On the station wagons only, the fuel filler cap returns to the left rear fender.

The script nameplate appears on the rear doors of the station wagons Brookwood and Yeoman station wagons. The Nomad has a Bel Air emblem and Nomad nameplate at the rear of its fenders.

Station wagons have a single tail light instead of the three used on passenger cars and their fenders have less "roll-over".

The wide lift gate now has a curved glass window.

Chevrolet script appears on the rear, matching the one on the hood. Above it, on the lift gate, is a new outside handle to aid in opening it. Also new is the pushbutton latch release replacing the locking handle of 1957 (page 257).

1958

With the smaller engines further from the radiator, a shroud is placed around the fan to aid cooling.

The valve covers of the 283 cubic inch Turbo-Fire engine bear the Chevrolet script.

The hood hinges have sturdy counter-balancing springs.

An accessory, the windshield washer is fed from this glass reservoir on the left side under the hood.

The rubber hose is part of subsequent required pollution equipment. It vents crankcase fumes into the carburetor through the air cleaner.

A tube brings hot air from the manifold to open the automatic choke.

The Generator is belt driven and mounted at the front left side of the engine.

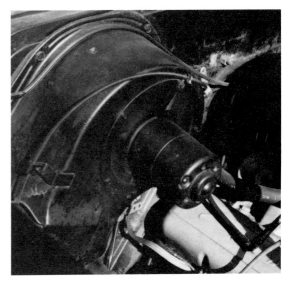

A plenum chamber under the hood works to deliver better air flow from the heater and ventilating system.

CHEVROLET '59

IMPALA SERIES
  4-door Sedan
  Convertible
  Sport Coupe   (2-door hardtop)
  Sport Sedan   (4-door hardtop)

BEL AIR SERIES
  2-door Sedan
  4-door Sedan
  Sport Sedan   (4-door hardtop)

BISCAYNE SERIES
  2-door Sedan
  4-door Sedan
  Utility Sedan   (2-door 3-passenger Sedan)

STATION WAGON SERIES
  Nomad   (4-door 6-passenger)
  Kingswood   (4-door 9-passenger)
  Parkwood   (4-door 6-passenger)
  Brookwood   (4-door 6-passenger)
  Brookwood   (2-door 6-passenger)

After only one year on the 117" wheelbase, 1959 saw the introduction of an entirely new X-frame 119" wheelbase chassis with an overall length increase of two inches to 210.9, some eleven inches longer than 1957. With all-new sheetmetal and some of the most unique styling that has ever appeared on the road, the 1959 Chevrolet was, as they claimed, "all new all over again!".

With a unique new slotted air intake just over the conventional front grill, and a pair of "cat's eye" rear tail lights, there was to be no mistaking the 1959 Chevrolet. The features were introduced with this model year and eliminated with the next for a truly unique reference.

The Impala, which last year was a sub-series of the Bel Air, became a full Series of its own, the top of the Chevrolet line. Bel Air Series became the mid-range, and was reduced to only three models. At the low-priced end, the former Delray Series name was abandoned, and Biscayne, last years mid-range, was the name assigned to them. The station wagons continued to rate a series of their own, and in the five-model selection, the name Nomad name continued to be found, again on a 4-door version.

The standard six-cylinder Blue Flame engine, now called the "Hi-Thrift 6" continued to be offered, along with the 283 cid V-8 which was rated at 185 horsepower in basic form and offered several optional modifications up to a fuel injected, 10.5:1 compression ratio maximum performance 290 horsepower model. In addition, the bigger 348 cid Turbo-Thrust V-8 had, in addition to its basic 4-barrel carburetor 250 horsepower version, a three two-barrel carburetor 315 horsepower option bringing the total engine selections up to eight.

New for 1958 was an optional 4-speed transmission which joined Powerglide, Overdrive, and Turboglide transmissions and Positraction (limited slip differential) Rear End to increase your opportunity to tailor your own vehicle.

specifications

engine

135-H.P. HI-THRIFT 6: 235.5 cu. in., 8.25:1 compression ratio, single-barrel carburetion, single exhaust. 185-H.P. TURBO-FIRE V8: 283 cu. in., 8.5:1 compression ratio, two-barrel carburetion, single exhaust (dual optional*). 230-H.P. SUPER TURBO-FIRE V8*: 283 cu. in., 9.5:1 compression ratio, four-barrel carburetion, single exhaust (dual optional*). 250-H.P. RAMJET FUEL INJECTION V8*: 283 cu. in., 9.5:1 compression ratio, Ramjet Fuel Injection, dual exhaust. 250-H.P. TURBO-THRUST V8*: 348 cu. in., 9.5:1 compression ratio, four-barrel carburetion, dual exhaust. 280-H.P. SUPER TURBO-THRUST V8*: 348 cu. in., 9.5:1 compression ratio, triple two-barrel carburetion, dual exhaust. 290-H.P. RAMJET SPECIAL V8*: 283 cu. in., 10.5:1 compression ratio, Ramjet Fuel Injection, dual exhaust. 320-H.P. TURBO-THRUST SPECIAL V8*: 348 cu. in., 11.25:1 compression ratio, four-barrel carburetion, dual exhaust (305 H.P., 11:1 compression ratio with Powerglide). 335-H.P., SUPER TURBO-THRUST SPECIAL V8*: 348 cu. in., 11.25:1 compression ratio, triple two-barrel carburetion, dual exhaust.

All Chevrolet engines feature valve-in-head design, aluminum pistons, forged steel crankshaft, replaceable-insert main and connecting rod bearings, full-pressure lubrication, harmonic balancer, 12-volt electrical system, positive-shift starter, automatic choke, 3-point mounting. Hydraulic valve lifters standard on all except special V8 engines. V8 engines feature independent operating mechanism for each valve, integral valve guides, chain-driven camshaft, five main bearings, paper element type air cleaner, full-flow oil filter* (standard with fuel injection, mandatory with special 348-cu.-in. engines), four-quart oil refill (without filter), and dual exhaust system with resonators (optional* on Turbo-Fire V8 and Super Turbo-Fire V8). Turbo-Thrust V8 and Super Turbo-Thrust V8 have precision machined-in-bore combustion chambers and free-flow valves. Hi-Thrift 6 engine has shaft-mounted rocker arms, replaceable valve guides, four main bearings, gear-driven camshaft, oil-wetted air cleaner, by-pass type oil filter*, five-quart oil refill (without filter). Special V8 engines include special camshaft and valve system with mechanical valve lifters, premium bearings, and other heavy-duty features.

transmission

TURBOGLIDE*—Five-element torque converter with pump, three turbines, and dual-pitch stator controlled by accelerator pedal. Two turbine-operated planetary gear sets. Single forward Drive range. Grade Retarder, powerful reverse, and positive parking lock. Selector sequence P-R-N-D-Gr.
POWERGLIDE*—Three-element torque converter (pump, turbine and stator) with automatically controlled planetary gears in Drive range, manually selected for low and reverse. Positive parking lock. Selector sequence P-R-N-D-L.
4-SPEED SYNCHRO-MESH*—Close-ratio 4-Speed Synchro-Mesh design, all forward speeds fully synchronized. Central floor-mounted short-stroke shift lever. Gear ratios: First 2.20:1, second 1.66:1, third 1.31:1, fourth 1:1, reverse 2.26:1.
OVERDRIVE*—3-Speed Synchro-Mesh plus 2-speed planetary overdrive, engaged semi-automatically above approximately 30 m.p.h. Downshift to direct drive by flooring accelerator. Lock-out control handle.
3-SPEED SYNCHRO-MESH—All helical gear Synchro-Mesh design with high torque capacity. Gear ratios matched to power team: V8 first 2.47:1, second 1.53:1, third 1:1, reverse 2.80:1; all Overdrive and with 6-cylinder engines first and reverse 2.94:1, second 1.68:1, third 1:1.

clutch

9½-inch diaphragm spring type with Hi-Thrift 6 engine. 10-inch semi-centrifugal diaphragm spring type with Turbo-Fire V8, Super Turbo-Fire V8 and Ramjet Fuel Injection V8 engines. 10½-inch semi-centrifugal diaphragm spring type with Turbo-Thrust V8 and Super Turbo-Thrust V8 engines. All clutches have cushioned disc and permanently lubricated throw-out bearing.

chassis

SAFETY-GIRDER FRAME—Low, rigid tunnel-center X-built. FULL COIL SUSPENSION—Four coil springs with double-acting shock absorbers and built-in levelizing control, front and rear. Independent front suspension with spherical joints, ride stabilizer bar on all except 6-cylinder Bel Air and Biscayne models. Four-link rear suspension with four rugged rubber-bushed control arms. WHEELS AND TIRES—14" wheels, 7.50 x 14 4-ply rating low-pressure blackwall tubeless tires (8.00 x 14 4-ply rating on Convertible and Station Wagons). BRAKES—Hydraulic, self-energizing 11" Safety-Master brakes with bonded linings, area 199.5 square inches. Foot-operated mechanical parking brakes, finger-tip release. STEERING—Forward-mounted Ball-Race gear, balanced relay linkage. Overall ratio 28:1 standard, 24:1 with power steering*. REAR AXLE—Hypoid, semi-floating, four ratios tailored to power teams. FUEL CAPACITY—Station Wagons, 17 gals. (Kingswood, 18 gals.), all others, 20 gals. ELECTRICAL—12-volt system, 54-plate battery (66-plate with special 348-cu.-in. V8 engines), 30-ampere generator.

body

STRUCTURE—All-welded Fisher Unisteel construction, sealed and insulated, 12-point mounting. EXTERIOR—Magic-Mirror acrylic lacquer finish, distinctive trim and identification for each series, horizontal dual headlights, directional signals, high-level air intake, concealed fuel filler. Safety *Plate* Glass in all windows. APPOINTMENTS—Single key locks, push-button door handles, crank-operated front vent windows, electric windshield wipers. INTERIOR—Luxurious combinations of nylon-faced fabric and vinyl upholstery (all vinyl in Convertible and Brookwood Station Wagons). Vinyl side trim and headlining (cloth headlining in Impala 4-door sedan, Bel Air and Biscayne models). 2-spoke 17" recessed-hub steering wheel and instrument panel distinctive for each series. Enclosed steering column.

dimensions

Wheelbase, 119". Front and rear tread, 60.3" and 59.3". Overall: length 210.9", width 79.9", height—Sport Sedan, Sport Coupe and Convertible 54.0", Sedans 56.0", Station Wagons 56.3".

optional equipment*

Power steering. Power brakes. Power windows**. Flexomatic 6-Way power front seat**. Power tailgate window**. Vented full wheel covers. Heavy-duty rear coil springs. Positraction rear axle. Heavy-duty clutch**. E-Z-Eye glass. Padded instrument panel. De luxe equipment, steering wheel and foam rubber front seat cushion for Biscayne and Brookwood models. Heater and defroster. Air conditioner**. Whitewall and 8.00 x 14 4-ply tires. Choice of radios. Dual exhaust**. Oil filter. Heavy-duty generator**. Heavy-duty battery. Two-speed electric windshield wiper and pushbutton windshield washer. Oil-bath air cleaner for Hi-Thrift 6 engine. Special equipment for police or taxicab service. Full line of accessory equipment.
*Optional at extra cost. **Availability determined by either model or equipment.

1959 Impala Sport Coupe

Mr. Michael J. Puksas, Jr., Tustin, California

Two narrow air intake scoops appear just above the grill.

Decorative protrusions emphasize the new grill.

The headlights are set lower in the fenders, just above the bumpers.

All models have the Chevrolet scripts on their hood, only the Impala Series also has the crossed flag ornament, and the six-cylinder cars omit the V-shaped emblem.

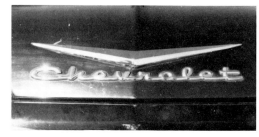

Dual headlamps are continued in a bright-metal frame placed low in the fenders.

These heavy chromed trim strips are used on the Impala and the Bel Air Series cars, but are omitted on the Biscayne Series and the two Brookwood Station Wagons.

Parking lamps, which also serve as directional signals, are built into these housings in the fender *above* the headlamps.

The round hard rubber bumpers are added accessories not found on the standard bumper (top photo).

The new windshield pillar and flat look of the rear fender give a distinctive look to the 1959 model.

A distinctive Impala trim stripe runs the length of the car.

Placed on the rear fender of the Impala Series, in the center of the special Impala stripe, is a distinctive crossed flag emblem (left) and behind it a lettered nameplate (lower left).

An entirely new, complexly curved, windshield now appears. With a compound curve at the ends and a similar curl near the top, it is a challenge to manufacturing skill.

Dual windshield wipers at the base of the windshield are electric operated.

The vent windows assume a new shape to match the needs of the new wrap-around windshield.

The appearance of the outside door handles is one of few unchanged items for 1959.

The rear window is widened and curves to meet a new narrow pillar.

Above the rear window, on the Impala Sport Coupe and Sport Sedan only, is a narrow simulated air vent. The roofline of the Sport Sedan extends out over the glass in similar fashion to that of the El Camino (page 307).

The "cat's eye" rear tail light is an exclusive mark of the 1959 Chevrolet.

Rear fenders roll over into a virtually flat upper surface.

The rear view of a 1959 Chevrolet is highly distinctive. Note that the tail pipes on this car have been changed. Originally they were oval.

The distinctive 1959 tail light housing conceals both parking light and stop light.

The vertical trim strips are used on the tail lights of the Impala Series cars only.

An additional trim stripe runs down the center of the rear deck on the Impala Series cars but is not used on the others.

The optional back-up lights are placed unobtrusively beneath the rear bumper.

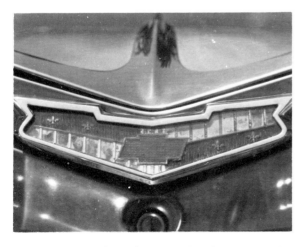

A new emblem whose shape matches the rear deck lid is used at its base. Below it can be seen the locking pushbutton release for the deck lid latch.

The special Impala steering wheel of 1958 is repeated for 1959, but this year the full-circle horn ring is shortened for better vision. Special trimmed foot pedals are used in Impalas.

A new, round, 120 mph speedometer appears in 1959. Directional signal indicators are placed at the ends of the scale.

The shift lever indicator for automatic transmissions, when used, is again located on the steering column at the base of the speedometer.

The decorative emblem at the center of the steering wheel is unchanged.

Again, three radio options are offered, each with either a front-or rear-mounted antenna. Below the center of the panel, is an ash receptacle.

On the new instrument panel, to the left of the speedometer, are gauges which show Generator or Oil Pressure mal-function, and coolant temperature. To the right, similar housings display Gasoline level, and accommodate an electric clock, standard in the Impala Series only.

An entirely new inside door "knob" is used in the Impala Series. Bel Air and Biscayne Series cars continue to use the earlier style (page 285).

A new nameplate appears for the ignition lock, but the functions are not changed.

Chevrolet's name appears, in block letters, on the right side of the instrument panel above a locking package compartment.

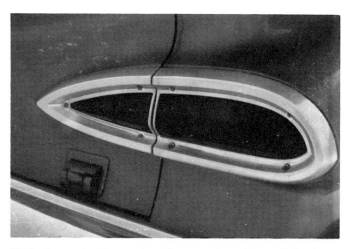

From the rear, even the station wagons are unmistakably 1959.

With the need to lower the tailgate, an ingenious split has been designed into station wagon tail lights.

1959 Parkwood Station Wagon

The rear window of the station wagons now retracts into the tailgate. To operate the window mechanism, the cap of the round emblem folds back (lower right photo) to provide a crank. The lock is for the tailgate latch *and* the window. The flap on which the emblem below the window crank is placed is hinged. Lifting it releases the tail gate.

Introduced by the truck division in 1959, the Chevrolet El Camino married the rugged pick-up truck's hauling ability with the comfort and convenience of a passenger car. Featuring a high fashion all-vinyl interior, passenger car instrument panel, carpeting, and wrapped-around glass for exceptional visibility, it also offered a pickup box that was over six feet long and almost 5½ feet wide. Double-walled side panels added protection, and a full-width fold-down tailgate make loading the all-steel ribbed floor of the El Camino an easy task.

The roof of the El Camino resembles that of the Impala Sport Sedan in that it over-hangs the rear glass considerably.

The passenger compartment of the El Camino features excellent visibility with glass wrapped around to narrow roof support pillars.

A wide door provides excellent access to the interior.

Although the trim plates below it are standard, the tie-down railing on this car is an accessory.

The steering wheel of the El Camino is not the special Impala wheel (page 302), but it does have a distinctive two-spoke design which it shares with the Bel Air Series cars.

The spare tire of the El Camino is ingeniously stored behind the hinged passenger seat.

From the rear, the El Camino greatly resembles the Station Wagon design on which it is based.

The pickup box walls are double-walled steel and the steel floor is ribbed for added strength.

The license plate is held on a hinged bracket so that it may remain in a vertical position when the tailgate is lowered (right).

The tailgate lowers for floor-level loading, and folding hinges are provided to support its ends.

With its 1959 models, Chevrolet brought the decade to a close. For over 20 years, the Division had led its competition, Ford, in passenger car production, and had seen the *intentions* of William Durant and the *instructions* of Alfred Sloan result in an unquestioned Leadership. For although even these two had possibly sought only to defeat Ford's claim to First Place, their goal was reached with units to spare, and Chevrolet's larger production not only placed it above Ford, but, according to records of the Automobile Manufacturer's Association, Chevrolet had, since 1946, produced *by itself* over 17,000,000 passenger cars, a figure equal to thirteen per cent more than Ford. More, it was almost 23% of the total number of cars produced by *all* domestic manufacturers during that period. Virtually one car out of 5 was a Chevrolet; truly it had become . . . CHEVROLET: USA #1.

WHEELCOVERS

1946-48

1949 (red centers)

1950 (gold centers)

1951

1952

1953 Two-Ten and One-Fifty Series hub cap (top photo) and Bel Air full wheelcover (right).

1954 Bel Air wheelcover and Hub Cap (top photo) used on Two-Ten and One-Fifty models.

1955 Bel Air full wheelcover.

1956 Bel Air full wheelcover (left), hub cap (above), and accessory wire wheel cover (right).

1957 Two-Ten and One-Fifty hub cap (above) and Bel Air wheelcover (right).

1957 accessory added spinner on wheelcover (left) and hub cap (below).

1958 hub cap (left), Impala/Bel Air wheel-cover (below) and accessory spinner on 1958 wheelcover (right).

1959 Full Wheelcover

SOME ACCESSORIES

It is the Author's intention neither to mislead nor misrepresent. The accessories shown here are representative of many found on the cars which were studied in preparing the material for this text. Some may not have actually been offered by Chevrolet, but, like some of the attractive rear view mirrors, may have originated with Western Auto. All are appropriate, however, to the enjoyment of the cars.

Not really "accessories" in the classic sense, attractive "USA #1" license plates were conceived by Chevrolet as dress-up items to be used in Dealer's Showrooms. Readily available, many find their way into the hands of Owners or Collectors who have noted the subtle annual changes in the plates.

Locking gas filler caps are GM accessories especially popular at times of gasoline shortage.

The Chevrolet No-Glare Inside Rear View Mirror is an excellent night-driving aid and dates from the early 'Fifties'.

The accessory back-up light on the rear splash apron of this 1949 Chevrolet is the same part as is used as a cowl light on the 1932 models.

Many Dealers provide special license plate holders bearing their names.

An accessory external sunvisor was available from Chevrolet through the early 1950's.

Many outside rear view mirror designs were offered by both the factory and also by the Dealers who added them before making delivery.

SOME ACCESSORIES

Several types of rear bumper accessory guards were offered. On the right, a 1953 model, below, a 1951.

The Chevrolet Vacu-Matic ash receiver operated through a vacuum line from the manifold and helped to prevent flying cigarette ashes.

Accessory dress-up gas filler door trim is available for both the earlier style (above) and the post-1955 front-hinged door. Fewer stripes appear on the fin of the earlier style.

In the early post-war years of shortages, wide white beauty rings were offered which simulated white-wall tires.

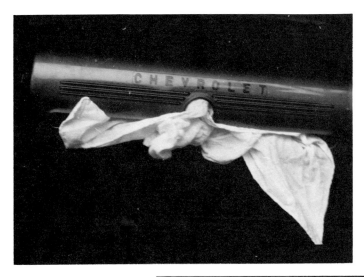

At least two types of genuine Chevrolet under-dash Kleenex dispensers were available.

A popular accessory, this rubber heel protector, slips over the accelerator and protects the mat below it.

Interesting after-market driving aids include a compass (above) and thermometer.

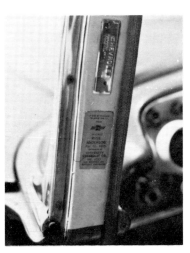

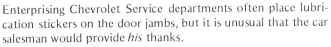

Enterprising Chevrolet Service departments often place lubrication stickers on the door jambs, but it is unusual that the car salesman would provide *his* thanks.

Unusual right-hand Sportlamp with integral rear-view mirror matches another on left side.

Under-hood, gravity-operated, lamp illuminates engine compartment when hood is raised.

BASIC ENGINE DATA & POWER TEAMS

1953

Engine	Models	Cu. In. Displ.	Comp. Ratio	Bore	Stroke	Gross H.P.	Net H.P.	Carburetor	Transmission
Thriftmaster	SDL.	216	6.6	3-1/2"	3-3/4"	92 @ 3400 RPM	85 @ 3300 RPM	Single Barrel	3-Speed
Conventional	PASS. (exc. SDL)	235	7.1	3-9/16"	3-15/16"	108 @ 3600 RPM	103 @ 3500 RPM	Single Barrel	3-Speed
Blue Flame	2100-2400	235	7.5	3-9/16"	3-15/16"	115 @ 3600 RPM	108 @ 3600 RPM	Single Barrel	Powerglide

1954-1955

Engine	Models	Cu. In. Displ.	Comp. Ratio	Bore	Stroke	Gross H.P.	Net H.P.	Carburetor	Transmission
Blue Flame 115	PASS.	235	7.5	3-9/16"	3-15/16"	115 @ 3700 RPM	107 @ 3600 RPM	Single Barrel	3-Speed
Blue Flame 125	PASS.	235	7.5	3-9/16"	3-15/16"	125 @ 4000 RPM	115 @ 3800 RPM	Single Barrel	Powerglide

1955

Engine	Models	Cu. In. Displ.	Comp. Ratio	Bore	Stroke	Gross H.P.	Net H.P.	Carburetor	Transmission
Blue Flame 123—6 cyl.	PASS.	235	7.5	3-9/16"	3-15/16"	123 @ 3800 RPM	109 @ 3600 RPM	Single Barrel	3-Speed Overdrive
Blue Flame 136—6 cyl.	PASS.	235	7.5	3-9/16"	3-15/16"	136 @ 4200 RPM	121 @ 3800 RPM	Single Barrel	Powerglide
Turbo-Fire 8 cyl.	PASS.	265	8.0	3-3/4"	3"	162 @ 4400 RPM	137 @ 4000 RPM	2-Barrel	3-Speed Overdrive Powerglide
Turbo-Fire 8 cyl.	PASS.	265	8.0	3-3/4"	3"	180 @ 4600 RPM	160 @ 4200 RPM	4-Barrel	3-Speed Overdrive Powerglide

1956

Engine	Models	Cu. In. Displ.	Comp. Ratio	Bore	Stroke	Gross H.P.	Net H.P.	Carburetor	Transmission
Blue Flame 140—6 cyl.	PASS.	235	8.0	3-9/16"	3-15/16"	140 @ 4200 RPM	125 @ 4000 RPM	Single Barrel	3-Speed Overdrive Powerglide
Turbo-Fire 162—8 cyl.	PASS.	265	8.0	3-3/4"	3"	162 @ 4400 RPM	137 @ 4000 RPM	2-Barrel	3-Speed Overdrive
Turbo-Fire 170—8 cyl.	PASS.	265	8.0	3-3/4"	3"	170 @ 4400 RPM	141 @ 4000 RPM	2-Barrel	Powerglide
Turbo-Fire 205—8 cyl.	PASS.	265	8.0	3-3/4"	3"	205 @ 4600 RPM	170 @ 4200 RPM	4-Barrel	3-Speed Overdrive Powerglide
Turbo-Fire 225—8 cyl.	PASS.	265	9.25	3-3/4"	3"	225 @ 5200 RPM	196 @ 4800 RPM	Dual 4-Barrel	3-Speed Overdrive Powerglide

1957

Engine	Models	Cu. In. Displ.	Comp. Ratio	Bore	Stroke	Gross H.P.	Net H.P.	Carburetor	Transmission
Blue Flame 140—6 cyl.	PASS.	235	8.0	3-9/16''	3-15/16''	140 @ 4200 RPM	125 @ 4000 RPM	Single-Barrel	3-Speed, OD, PG
Turbo-Fire 265—8 cyl.	PASS.	265	8.0	3-3/4''	3''	162 @ 4400 RPM	137 @ 4000 RPM	2-Barrel	3-Speed Overdrive
Turbo-Fire 283—8 cyl.	PASS.	283	8.5	3-7/8''	3''	185 @ 4600 RPM	150 @ 4200 RPM	2-Barrel	Powerglide Turboglide
Super Turbo-Fire 283—8 cyl.	PASS.	283	9.5	3-7/8''	3''	220 @ 4800 RPM	190 @ 4600 RPM	4-Barrel	3-Speed, OD, A.T.
8 Cylinder	PASS.	283	9.5	3-7/8''	3''	245 @ 5000 RPM	215 @ 4800 RPM	Dual 4-Barrel	3-Speed, Close-Ratio, A.T.
8 Cylinder	PASS.	283	9.5	3-7/8''	3''	250 @ 5000 RPM	225 @ 4800 RPM	Fuel Injection	3-Speed, Close-Ratio, A.T.
*8 Cylinder	PASS.	283	9.5	3-7/8''	3''	270 @ 6000 RPM	230 @ 6000 RPM	Dual 4-Barrel	3-Speed, Close-Ratio
*8 Cylinder	PASS.	283	10.5	3-7/8''	3''	283 @ 6200 RPM	240 @ 5600 RPM	Fuel Injection	3-Speed, Close-Ratio

1958

Engine	Models	Cu. In. Displ.	Comp. Ratio	Bore	Stroke	Gross H.P.	Net H.P.	Carburetor	Transmission
Blue Flame 145—6 cyl.	PASS.	235.5	8.25	3-9/16''	3-15/16''	145 @ 4200 RPM	125 @ 4000 RPM	Single Barrel	3-Speed, OD, PG
Turbo-Fire 283—8 cyl.	PASS.	283	8.5	3-7/8''	3''	185 @ 4600 RPM	150 @ 4200 RPM	2-Barrel	3-Speed, OD, A.T.
Super Turbo-Fire 283—8 cyl.	PASS.	283	9.5	3-7/8''	3''	230 @ 4800 RPM	175 @ 4400 RPM	4-Barrel	3-Speed, OD, PG
Ramjet Fuel Injection—8 cyl.	PASS.	283	9.5	3-7/8''	3''	250 @ 5000 RPM	225 @ 4800 RPM	Fuel Injection	3-Speed, A.T.
*Ramjet Fuel Injection—8 cyl.	PASS.	283	10.5	3-7/8''	3''	290 @ 6200 RPM	245 @ 5600 RPM	Fuel Injection	3-Speed
Turbo-Thrust 348—8 cyl.	PASS.	348	9.5	4-1/8''	3-1/4''	250 @ 4400 RPM	210 @ 4400 RPM	4-Barrel	3-Speed A.T.
Super Turbo-Thrust 348—8 cyl.	PASS.	348	9.5	4-1/8''	3-1/4''	280 @ 4800 RPM	235 @ 4800 RPM	3/2 Barrel	3-Speed, Turboglide
*Super Turbo-Thrust 348—8 cyl.	PASS.	348	11.0	4-1/8''	3-1/4''	315 @ 5600 RPM	—	3/2 Barrel	3-Speed

*MAXIMUM performance engines have special performance-type camshaft, high-speed valve system and mechanical valve lifters. All other engines have hydraulic valve lifters.

1959

Engine	Models	Cu. In. Displ.	Comp. Ratio	Bore	Stroke	Gross H.P.	Net H.P.	Carburetor	Transmission
Hi-Thrift 135—6 cyl.	PASS.	283	8.25	3-9/16''	3-15/16''	135 @ 4000 RPM	115 @ 3600 RPM	Single Barrel	3-Speed, OD, PG
Turbo-Fire 283—8 cyl.	PASS.	283	8.5	3-7/8''	3''	185 @ 4600 RPM	150 @ 4200 RPM	2-Barrel	3-Speed, OD, A.T.
Super Turbo-Fire 283—8 cyl.	PASS.	283	9.5	3-7/8''	3''	230 @ 4800 RPM	175 @ 4400 RPM	4-Barrel	3-Speed, OD, A.T.
▲Ramjet Fuel Injection 283—8 cyl.	PASS.	283	9.5	3-7/8''	3''	250 @ 5000 RPM	225 @ 4800 RPM	Fuel Injection	3 or 4-Speed, A.T.
●Ramjet Fuel Injection 283—8 cyl.	PASS.	283	10.5	3-7/8''	3''	290 @ 6200 RPM	245 @ 5600 RPM	Fuel Injection	3 or 4-Speed
Turbo-Thrust 348—8 cyl.	PASS.	348	9.5	4-1/8''	3-1/4''	250 @ 4400 RPM	210 @ 4400 RPM	4-Barrel	3 or 4-Speed, A.T.
▲Super Turbo-Thrust 348—8 cyl.	PASS.	348	9.5	4-1/8''	3-1/4''	280 @ 4800 RPM	235 @ 4800 RPM	3/2 Barrel	3 or 4-Speed, A.T.
●Special Turbo-Thrust 348—8 cyl.	PASS.	348	11.0	4-1/8''	3-1/4''	305 @ 5600 RPM	—	4-Barrel	3 or 4-Speed, P.G.
●Special Super Turbo-Thrust 348—8 cyl.	PASS.	348	11.0	4-1/8''	3-1/4''	315 @ 5600 RPM	—	3/2 Barrel	3 or 4-Speed
●Special Turbo-Thrust 348—8 cyl.	PASS.	348	11.25	4-1/8''	3-1/4''	320 @ 5600 RPM	—	4-Barrel	3 or 4-Speed
●Special Super Turbo-Thrust 348—8 cyl.	PASS.	348	11.25	4-1/8''	3-1/4''	345 @ 5600 RPM	—	3/2 Barrel	3 or 4-Speed

PRODUCTION FIGURES

For several reasons it is difficult accurately to determine the passenger car production figures for the major Companies. Many tables include trucks and busses as well as other commercial chassis. Sometimes the figures are over-stated, other times they appear to be understated for no apparent reason.

The Author has analyzed data from several sources including the General Motors Annual Reports, the figures published in Moody's Industrial Manual, Wards Automotive yearbooks, tables included in "My Years with General Motors" by Alfred P. Sloan, Jr., and Nevins & Hill's excellent "Ford: Decline and Rebirth", as well as Ford's own raw data and the statistics published by the Automobile Manufacturers Association.

The figures herein presented represent a compilation and weighted consideration of all of the above.

Comparison of Passenger Vehicle Production*

	FORD	CHEVROLET	
1946	372,917	397,109	+ 7%
1947	601,665	695,992	+ 17%
1948	549,077	775,990	+ 41%
1949	841,170	1,109,958	+ 32%
1950	1,187,076	1,520,583	+ 28%
1951	900,770	1,118,101	+ 24%
1952	777,531	877,950	+ 13%
1953	1,185,185	1,477,299	+ 25%
1954	1,394,762	1,414,365	+ 1%
1955	1,764,524	1,830.038	+ 4%
1956	1,373,542	1,621,018	+ 18%
1957	1,522,408	1,522,549	—
1958	1,038,560	1,255,943	+ 21%
1959	1,528,592	1,428,980	- 6%
	15,036,775	17,045,875	+ 13%

*Figures relate to the number of vehicles produced in the calendar year and do not necessarily relate to number of vehicles *sold*.

For additional information on the subject,
Readers may be interested in contacting:

Vintage Chevrolet Club of America
P.O. Box 5387
Orange, California 92667

Classic Chevy Club
P.O. Box 17188
Orlando, Florida 32810

National Nomad Club
P.O. Box 606
Arvada, Colorado 80001